THE HIDDEN TREASURES IN HEBREWS

Heroes of Faith

AN INDUCTIVE BIBLE STUDY BY
EVELYN WHEELER

P.O. Box 2067
Eugene, Oregon 97402

Scripture verses in this book are taken from the New American Standard Bible ®, Copyright © 1960, 1962, 1963, 1968, 1971, 1972, 1973, 1975, 1977, 1995 by the Lockman Foundation. Used by permission.

Truth Trackers: The Hidden Treasures in Hebrews
Copyright © 2004 by Evelyn Wheeler
Published by Liberty Books
P.O. Box 23537
Richfield, Minnesota 55423

ISBN 978-1-886930-28-5

All rights reserved. No part of this book may be reproduced in any form or by any means without written permission from the publisher.

Printed in the United States of America.

Contents

Introduction: The Hidden Treasures of the Bible 5

1. Our Adventure Begins! 7
2. The Power of Faith 21
3. Abel and the Obedience of Faith 35
4. Enoch and the Devotion of Faith 47
5. Noah and a Trusting Faith 57
6. Abraham and His Believing Faith 69
7. Sarah's Confident Faith 83
8. Joseph's Steadfast Faith 91
9. Moses' Fearless Faith 107
10. Rahab's Faith of Abandon 121
11. David's Patient Faith 133
12. Jesus: Author and Perfecter of OUR Faith 147

    Treasure Map 159

    Key to Games 163

To my mom,

who is my hero,

who has, by her example, taught me to be constant, to be giving, and to be a person of my word.

Hidden Treasures of the Bible

Welcome to a study about an amazing topic from the Bible: faith. You're joining a great group of kids called Truth Trackers who are always digging in search of the truth of the Word of God!

Our study is like a great archaeological dig! Archaeologists are people who dig through the remains of old civilizations to understand how men, women, and children lived thousands of years ago. As they piece together bits of the past that they unearth, they eventually get a bigger picture of what life was like.

Like archaeologists, we are going to dig into the Bible to see what we can discover about faith. Below the surface of the passages we will dig through, you will discover many truths and treasures. Together we're going to dig and sift and sort through these Bible verses so that you can come away with truths that will help you for the rest of your life. Yes, the great thing about the dig is you'll get a bigger picture too—a picture of what God is saying to you about some important issues for life.

Before you start, meet a friendly camel named Clayton. His ancestors lived in Bible times, so he has heard all the stories of the Bible as they have been passed down from generation to generation. He even had a distant uncle in Bethlehem the night Jesus was born! Clayton will be the head archaeologist on this exciting adventure! He'll talk you through each dig.

As you begin this incredible dig on the topic of faith, remember that archaeologists work very long, hard hours. They have very exciting jobs, and the result of their work is very rewarding! But it is not easy work! Remember, too, that you can't unearth the treasures in the Bible without lots of work!

You won't discover the kind of truths we are after by sitting in front of the television or staring at your computer. You must get up, grab your boots, hat, and tools and dig into the Word. You have to push through all five layers of each dig to understand everything God wants to say to you. It won't happen if you don't get up, dig in, and do your part.

There will be many, many times throughout your life that you'll be glad you spent this time digging in the Bible because you'll know what God says and what He wants. And then you'll be able to do the right thing and please Him! At the end of our twelve digs, you'll have a treasure chest full of truth that will help you all your life.

We're almost ready to get started digging. First, let me tell you some "rules of the road":

Tools of the Trade: At the beginning of each lesson is a list of tools you'll need in order to complete the lesson. You should always gather these together before you begin the work. Like a good archaeologists, you need the right tools to get the job done.

 **Directions for Diggers:** This short section is the introduction to each dig and gives you an idea of the dig's topic. Remember that on any dig there is a head archaeologist who directs the dig, so Clayton will talk you through this brief section.

Chart the Course: You'll have a chance to work on some charts that will help you understand the material. At a dig site, there is a graph or map that shows the team where to dig. The charts in your study will point the way to truth treasures for you! Whenever you see a map, be sure you look at it to find the locations mentioned in the work you're doing that day.

Clues: As you work through the digs, from time to time you'll be given clues that will help you unearth truth. Every site has clues that point to where special treasures can be discovered. You'll be given clues to point you to truth as you work.

Treasure Map: It is easier to find treasures if you have a master map of the area where you're working. Chapter 11 from the book of Hebrews sometimes is called the faith hall of fame, and it will be your master map for this dig. I call it the "Treasure Map" because through the study of Hebrews 11, you'll discover GREAT treasures. This chapter is printed at the back of your study book.

Checking in with Headquarters: Each time you begin a new dig, you should pray and ask the Holy Spirit to teach you truth. Just like on a dig when everyone checks in with the head guy for directions for the day, you should check in for help with your study.

Truth Treasures for the Week: At the end of each week's dig, you'll see a place for you to record three truth treasures you discovered. On an archaeological dig, when a section of the dig is complete, all of the finds are tagged and information about each is noted. In the same way, you'll tag some key truths and note them. Be sure not to skip this section! You're on your own when it comes to this part, but it is very important!

Bury the Treasure: One of the wisest things you can do is to memorize the Word of God. Each dig has a special treasure that you'll unearth, and you'll want to bury it in your heart by memorizing it.

Puzzles: Throughout the study, you'll find a variety of fun puzzles that will help you review the truth you're learning. It is kind of like being on a dig and watching as the head archaeologist tries to put broken pieces together to see if they have discovered a table, a jar, a bowl, or who knows what! It'll be fun to work through these and see what you discover! (A key to each puzzle can be found at the back of the book so that you can check your answers.)

**Well, you're prepared. Are you ready to go? I hope so.
Take off to Dig One. Clayton will meet you there.**

Dig 1

Our Adventure Begins!

Tools of the Trade

1. Colored pencils
2. Pen or pencil
3. Treasure Map of the sections from the gospels on pages 159-161
4. Chart: A Look At Hebrews 11–12:3 on page 17-18
5. Game on page 19

Directions for Diggers

Have you ever heard people talk about faith? I've heard my great grandfather say, "I have the faith to believe the good Lord will send the rain we need." But I never really understood exactly what "GG" meant by this. (Yes, I call him GG. Of course, that is short for "great grandfather." He likes it!)

I only knew that in the desert where we live we are always grateful for rain! Even though I can carry lots of water in the hump on my back and go for a long time without

much water, I know the land itself needs water in order for food to grow and for the water supply to stay at a good level.

But when I would walk home from the little village where GG lives, my mind could not stop trying to figure out what faith had to do with whether it would rain or not. So one day when I heard GG make his declaration, I asked about faith.

He immediately sat me down and began to talk with me. It was hard to get what he was saying since faith isn't something I could see or touch. In fact, the more he talked, the more I wondered why anyone would put so much confidence in something that seemed invisible and so far away from our little world.

I realized that I couldn't go to the store and buy it. I couldn't borrow it from my friend. I couldn't turn on the television and see it. And my mom couldn't make it in her kitchen. So, what was the big deal about faith? It didn't seem very useful to me because I couldn't even touch it.

Then one day as I read a book in the Bible called Hebrews, I came to a part that seemed to be all about faith. So I took some time to think about what these verses were saying. And I think that spending some time really looking at Hebrews 11–12:3 helped me make sense out of something that had seemed like the air to me—something I couldn't grab on to—before. Now I understand that faith is important. And I know, too, that it is something we should all have in our hearts! But, as I said before, you can't just go buy some for yourself.

Good news though! Even though you can't pick up a box of faith the next time you are out shopping with your mom, I think if you will spend some time with me looking at these verses that you, too, will get a grip on a topic that may seem just like empty space to you at this moment. It may sound a bit boring to be talking about studying faith, but I can tell you that is where you are really wrong, wrong, wrong. I mean so wrong that you may miss the boat if you don't come on this dig!

I am excited and proud of you for being willing to stretch your brain and for being willing to take time to really dig in and understand this topic! The time you will spend now will really pay off in the end. So let's get started in our study. You'll see that studying the Bible can be a lot of fun. It may seem like a lot of work sometimes too, but don't give up. Ask God to help you to be the best student you can be. And ask Him to fill your tank with faith, even if you don't understand exactly what it means yet. He will be glad to do just that!

And here is a clue to help you get off to a great start: **Clue #1:** It will be much easier if you work on a dig one layer at a time. Just dig through one layer each day instead of trying to work through an entire dig in one sitting.

LAYER ONE: Checking in with Headquarters

Before we head off for a day of digging for truth, let me remind you of something and give you an idea about what our dig will be like. Okay, here we go! We are off and running!

Our Adventure Begins!

1. When I read the Word of God, sometimes I understand exactly what I read. Other times, although I know all of the words, when I look at the sentence and see all of the words together, I don't know what is being said. It seems strange to know all of the words in a sentence and not get what they mean when they are all used together, doesn't it?

But my guess is that you have had the same experience! Know what I do when I can't understand what the Word of God is saying? I ask for help! And then when I go back and take my time and examine carefully what is written, I usually get an idea about the meaning.

Do you know that *you* can get extra help to understand the Word of God? Great news, isn't it? Well, in John 16:13, the Bible says, "But when He, the Spirit of truth, comes, He will guide you into all truth…." This verse is a promise to you that the Holy Spirit will help you understand the truth that God has in the Bible!

You can think of it in this way: When you take swimming or ballet lessons and you come to a stroke or a position you can't master or can't remember, you can ask your instructor for help. Because the instructor understands the skills you need, he or she can help you!

Well, when you pray and ask the Holy Spirit for help, it is like asking your instructor for help. And in the same way that your teacher or instructor helps you, the Holy Spirit will lead you to the answer—to the truth!

So if you can't understand or figure out what you read in this study or in your Bible, you can pray and ask for help. God wants you to understand! And the good news is that He *always* knows the answer and He is *never* too busy to listen and help! Sometimes He will show you the answer right away, and sometimes it may take some time for Him to help you see the answer. But He will show you.

Do you remember that we are calling our prayer time for help in understanding the Word of God "checking in with headquarters"? You should check in each day before you begin digging. You wouldn't start an important archeological dig without checking in with the head archeologists for directions, would you? Well, you also don't want to dig into God's Word without asking for the help of the Holy Spirit, your teacher and guide.

2. Do you and your family ever work on jigsaw puzzles together? One of my friends really likes to work puzzles. I like them too, but sometimes when we pour all one thousand of those little pieces out on the table, the thought that we can connect them together to make a picture almost seems too much to believe. And sometimes the task of sitting for hours and trying to match jagged edges seems too difficult and too time consuming!

But when the popcorn is popped, the apple juice is poured, and a good CD is playing, what seemed like hard work minutes earlier now seems like fun. It is awfully fun, too, when all of those little pieces begin to fit together and form a picture! As we work and work and work on the puzzle, and study each piece to see how it fits together with the others, I always see more detail of the picture we are putting together than I did when I first looked at the lid of the box. Of course, I always have the lid from the box close by so I can keep looking at the finished picture—the big picture. It helps to have an idea of what all the pieces will look like when we finally get them together!

Studying a topic from God's Word can be like working a puzzle. You have to take a look at the topic to see the big picture, then you pour out lots of pieces and work to put them together. When, in the end, you have all your pieces connected, you see the big picture again. But because of all the work you have done to connect the pieces you understand more about the topic than you did when you just took your first look at the big picture. Also, because of all the work you have invested in understanding the topic, you see more of the details of the picture than you ever could have at your first glance.

This week we are going to begin looking at one of the most important topics in the Word of God. Yes, it is the topic of faith. As we begin, we are going to take a glance at a big picture of faith.

Once we see this big picture, then we will open the lid to the box and pour out the pieces. Next, day after day, week after week, as we head off on our digs, we will examine these pieces and fit them together. And as hard as it may seem to believe today, as you work to fit the pieces together you will begin to see a big picture about faith—and, because of your hard work, you will understand the details of the topic. It will be just like putting a puzzle together!

Are you ready? Your assignment for today will be to read pages 159-161 in the back of the book. These pages have some verses from the book of Hebrews printed out for you, and it is called your "Treasure Map." It is the treasure from the Word of God we are going to be digging through for the next few days! Hope you are rested and ready to go. This is a major dig!

This part of the book of Hebrews talks about faith, and by starting with these verses we will get a look at the big picture of this topic. You will see as you read that they have lots of our puzzle pieces in them! You will notice too that you are reading Hebrews chapter 11 and the first three verses of Hebrews 12.

To make these verses easier to work with, I have divided them into sections. You can tell where a section begins because I made the number of the verse that begins a new section big and bold!

Ask one of your parents, an older brother or sister, or an older friend to read pages 159-161 out loud to you. While they read, you can read silently with them. Reading through these verses will help you see how exciting our topic of faith is going to be. And you will also get a glimpse of the big picture that you are about to begin to piece together!

Don't worry if you don't understand some of what you read. Just keep reading. Have you ever heard the joke, "How do you eat a whale?" The answer is, "One bite at a time!" Of course, the point is that when something seems too big to even imagine how you will ever do it, you just do one thing at a time. Pretty bad joke, isn't it?

But, in the case of this study, the point of the joke is a good thing for us to remember. We have a lot of material to cover—material that will teach us about one of the most amazing truths of the Bible! So we must take one step at a time to cover all that we want to learn. And the first step is reading these scriptures that will give you a big picture about our topic.

So read the passage from Hebrews out loud with a family member or friend. After you finish the entire reading, you're all done for the day!

I am excited about what I know you will learn today. Take your time as you read. You will see the topic of faith clearly in chapter 11, but you may wonder why you are reading three verses from chapter 12. Think hard as you read, and we will talk about it all soon. Remember: Think BIG PICTURE—like the picture on the lid of the puzzle box!

LAYER TWO: The Big Picture

Yesterday you read through the verses from Hebrews about faith. Now you have a good idea of how important our topic is, and you saw how important God thinks it is for men and women to live by faith.

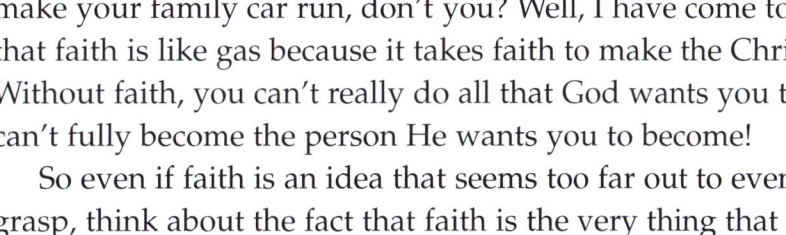

I understand you may feel that it is pointless to study something that seems to not even exist! It is hard to imagine how you can understand something that can't be seen, felt, heard, or *especially* that can't be eaten! But, now that I see more what faith is about, I know that it is essential for you to understand it! And I know you *can* understand it!

Let me tell you how I think about faith now that I understand it a little better. I think my idea may help you as we begin to discuss the topic. I have come to realize that faith is like gasoline. You know that it takes gasoline—fuel—to make your family car run, don't you? Well, I have come to understand that faith is like gas because it takes faith to make the Christian life run! Without faith, you can't really do all that God wants you to do, and you can't fully become the person He wants you to become!

So even if faith is an idea that seems too far out to even begin to grasp, think about the fact that faith is the very thing that will help you be God's man or God's woman! Now, that fact alone should make you rush to get your Bible and tear into this dig—and all of the digs that follow!

So, to keep this idea in terms we all understand, think about this idea: To begin this study, you need to back up your car and take off your gas cap because we are going to fill your tank with a truth that will energize your Christian life. Yes, we are going to fill your tank with faith! And because you will see that faith is the fuel you need to live a great Christian life, you will never let your tank get empty again!

A lot of the verses in Hebrews chapter 11 talked about men and women who lived their lives by faith. You see, too, that God honored these men and women by noting their faith in His Word. Have you ever had your teacher use your name as an example, or have you seen your name in the paper when you got a base hit or had a part in a school play? It feels good, doesn't it? It makes you feel important, and it lets you realize that someone was watching and knew you did a good job! Can you imagine what it would be like to have God use you as an example in His Word—a good example of a person who had faith! AWESOME!

1. Did you wonder why I had you read those three verses from chapter 12? Look back at these verses if you need to. Any ideas? Write your thoughts below.

Yes, chapter 12 talks about someone who made it possible for you to have faith! Jesus opened a way for you to have faith. We will talk more later about how.

2. Now that you have a view of the big picture of the topic of faith, let's open the puzzle box and pour out all of the pieces. Yes, the fun begins!

We will take our time and begin one piece at a time to work on our topic. We have lots and lots of pieces to examine and piece together. If you think popcorn and apple juice will help you, take a second and fix some. But don't take too long because I am eager to get started!

Now, grab your picks and let's dig around for a closer look—one passage at a time. Awesome, we're off!

Turn to your "Treasure Map" in the back of the book where the passage from Hebrews is printed out for you (pages 159-161) and read through this again. Now you'll be reading it yourself. If you read out loud, you'll remember it better.

3. Next find the chart called "A Look at Hebrews 11–12:3" at the end of this lesson (page 17). This chart will help you "chart the course." Look at the chart and find the column called "Titles." In that column are possible titles for this small section from Hebrews.

Our Adventure Begins!

You are going to take some time now and think about what you have read on the topic of faith. Usually when I work on one of these charts, I look at the entire book and then title each chapter. But because we are working with only a chapter and a few verses of another chapter, we are going to work with blocks of verses. I think working this way will help you the most. Okay, let's move forward!

First you should decide on a title for what we are calling section 1. It is Hebrews 11:1-3. If you need to, look back to the "Treasure Map" and see what these verses say. Then decide which of the titles you see on the chart is the best for these verses. Circle the title you think is the best.

Clue #2: Your title should tell you what the author talks about the most in that section. It should also help you remember what you read.

3. Now do the very same thing for the next section as you have done for the first. This section is 11:4-7 on your chart.

4. Now you get to be an artist! Hope you like to draw as much as I do! Don't worry if you don't feel very artistic. I mainly use stick figures when I draw people because I am not a great artist, but I like to try. I am pretty good with flowers, clouds, and grass, though! So, just try your best and enjoy yourself. If you don't have your colored pencils, run and get them. You're going to do an illustration.

An illustration is a picture used to explain something. Story books and comic books use lots of illustrations. The artist draws a picture to show your eyes the meaning of the words that you're reading. As you can see, there are illustrations of me, Clayton the Camel, all through this Bible study book. If you haven't met me before in one of the other studies, you can call me Clay for short. If you have done a study before, you already know all about me, and I hope you will be patient as I fill in the new students.

It's lots of fun to draw illustrations! Ready? Go back to the chart on page 17. In the column called "Illustrations," beside the title of the first section, draw what you think will remind you of the words that are in this section. You don't have to draw everything that you read about, just draw a sketch that will help you remember.

5. Now, that was fun, wasn't it? I just love to draw! Move ahead now and sketch your illustration for section 2, that is, verses 11:4-7.

Have fun drawing your illustration! I'll see you when we dig into Layer Three!

LAYER THREE: Tracking the Treasure

1. What does a good student of the Bible do before beginning to dig into the truth of the Word of God? If you said "pray," you're right! So take a moment and check in with headquarters. Ask the Holy Spirit to help you understand what God is saying to you in His Word.

2. Now turn to the "Treasure Map" at the back of the book (pages 159-161) and read through the entire passage from Hebrews again. As you read, remember to think about what you are seeing in each of the sections. That will help you to choose your title and draw a great illustration.

3. Now do as you did last layer and decide on your titles for sections 3 and 4.

4. Next, I want you to be an artist again today. Do exactly what you did in Layer Two when you worked on the chart at the end of the lesson—only this time work on sketches for sections 3 and 4. You may have a little harder time with your sketch for section 4, but I know when you think about it for a few moments you will think of what you can do. I realize it may be a bit difficult to see what this section means to the rest of the material.

Don't get bogged down in what you can't understand. Remember we are just examining pieces of the puzzle. We have not started trying to piece them together! We are just looking and seeing what we have to work with. Catch you tomorrow.

LAYER FOUR: Charting Your Course

Are you getting excited about the fact that you are learning about one of the most important topics of God's Word? Well, I hope you are! It is exciting stuff, and I think you will get more excited on each dig—because it keeps getting better as we dig out more truth and examine it!

1. Take out your pick again today and dig into sections 5 and 6. Again, don't get bogged down in trying to understand all the parts or pieces. We are just picking them up and looking at them to see where they may fit into our puzzle later.

Do you have your colored pencils? Turn back to page 18 and continue to "chart your course" by choosing your title and drawing your illustrations for sections 5 and 6.

Our Adventure Begins!

Your illustration for section 6 will be fun because you won't have any problem coming with some good ideas for it!

After you finish your work today, take a break from a hot day of digging. I know you have been sitting with me for a while. Maybe a bike ride sounds good. It does to me. See you at the beginning of Layer Five! Oh, yeah, don't forget to try your hand at the puzzle on page 19.

LAYER FIVE: Working on a Foundation

Have you ever seen a new house being built in your neighborhood? Or have you seen a new building being built in your town? Well, if you think about what you saw, you will remember that before any of the walls go up, there is a foundation put in place.

The base of the foundation is usually dug deep into the ground and is made of very strong materials like concrete and steel. The foundation is very important because if it is not prepared just right and if it is not strong enough, the house or building will not be able to stand for a long time.

That is what we have been doing in this dig! We have been laying a foundation so that you have a very strong base on which to build the truths about faith!

So, as you finish today, remember you are building a foundation!

1. Today, you'll dig into the last two sections of our passage! Can you believe you are to the bottom layer of our first dig? You've done a great job to be at this point.

Remember not to be concerned if you are not understanding all that you are digging through. We are just examining our puzzle pieces. In the digs to come, we will start connecting the treasures we unearth. It will become very, very exciting as you see an awesome and amazing picture take shape in your mind!

2. Okay, look at your chart on page 18 and think about your titles for the last two sections. Section 7 is really incredible because it talks about us! Won't you be looking forward to hearing more about these verses since we are mentioned in them? Section 8 is even more awesome because it talks mainly about Jesus. You are going to be blown away when we look closely at this section in one of our upcoming digs!

Well, enough from me. Title your sections!

3. Now, it is time to draw your last two sketches. Enjoy!

You're amazing! You have made it through Dig One, and I am proud of you. You should be proud of yourself, too. Mostly, you should be excited that you are in the process of

learning about one of the most important topics in the Word of God. Remember, it is the fuel for the Christian life! Don't you want to say, "Fill 'er up"?

See you at Dig Two. Now take a good break and have some fun! Oh, yeah, don't forget to record your three "Truth Treasures" from this dig! It should be very easy since you've been digging in such awesome verses from Hebrews.

Truth Treasures for the Week

1.

2.

3.

Bury the Treasure:

Now faith is the assurance of things hoped for, the conviction of things not seen. (Hebrews 11:1)

Our Adventure Begins!

A Look at Hebrews 11–12:3

Titles	Illustrations
Section 1: Hebrews 11:1-3	
Faith makes the invisible visible	
Faith gives us purpose	
Section 2: Hebrews 11:4-7	
Faith pleases God	
Faith makes us good people	
Section 3: Hebrews 11:8-12	
Abraham obeyed but did not know	
Abraham hoped he heard God	
Section 4: Hebrews 11:13-16	
They set their hearts on heaven	
They wanted a nicer place to live	

Titles	Illustrations
Section 5: Hebrews 11:17-31	
By faith…	
Mighty works by hoping in God	
Section 6: Hebrews 11:32-38	
Of Whom the world was not worthy	
Men and women who lived in caves	
Section 7: Hebrews 11:39-40	
Approval through faith	
Hope for approval at the end of life	
Section 8: Hebrews 12:1-3	
Jesus, the author and perfecter of faith	
Jesus sits beside God	

Our Adventure Begins!

Search and Decipher

In the following word hunt, find the names of the ten Heroes of Faith you discovered in the treasure map. I'll list them here to remind you of their names:

Abel	**Enoch**	**Noah**	**Abraham**	**Sarah**
Joseph	**Moses**	**Rahab**	**David**	**Jesus**

After you've circled all ten Heroes, place the remaining, uncircled letters on the spaces at the bottom of the page, starting at the arrow and moving from left to right to the bottom. But watch out for the Xs! They do not belong, and they are traps to get you off track. Once you've transferred all the letters, the message will tell you what these heroes of faith are for us. Good luck on your hunt!

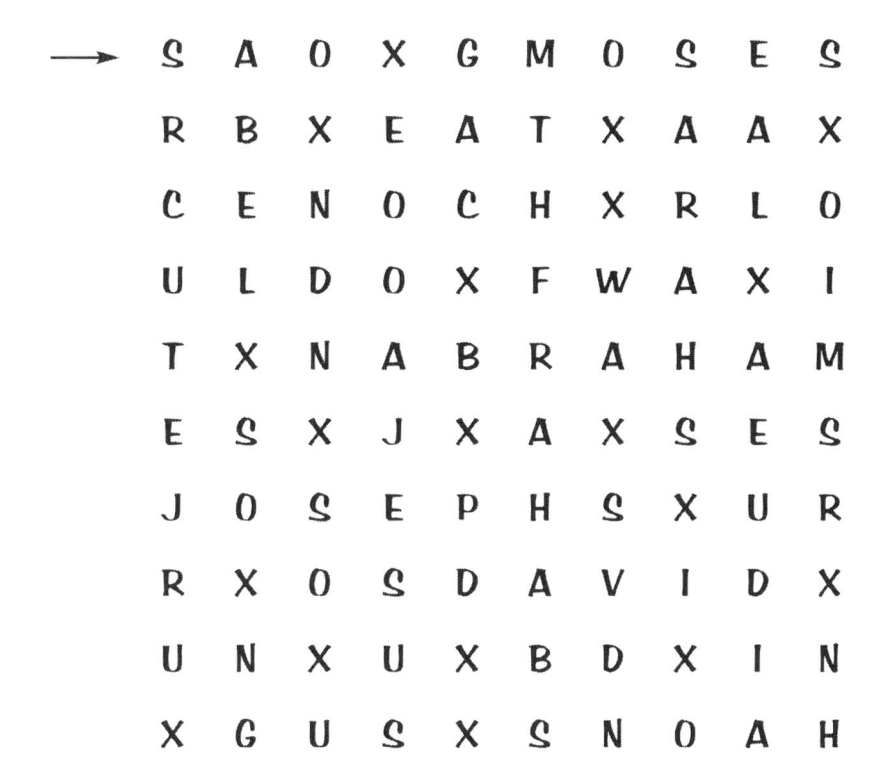

→ S A O X G M O S E S
   R B X E A T X A A X
   C E N O C H X R L O
   U L D O X F W A X I
   T X N A B R A H A M
   E S X J X A X S E S
   J O S E P H S X U R
   R X O S D A V I D X
   U N X U X B D X I N
   X G U S X S N O A H

"… __ __ __ __ __ __ __ __ __
    __ __ __ __ __ __ __
    __ __ __ __ __ __ __ __
    __ __ __ __ __ __ __ __ __ __ __ …"

solution on page 163

Dig 2

The Power of Faith

Tools of the Trade

1. Colored pencils
2. Pen or pencil
3. Dictionary
4. Game on page 33

Directions for Diggers

Have you fully recovered from our last dig? It took us a while to get to the bottom of those layers, didn't it? But you were great to hang in there, and I hope you are excited about all the treasure you unearthed!

This dig is going to be every bit as exciting as our last one, but this time you are going to dig for the treasures in a little different way.

Remember that we talked about puzzle pieces and how taking each one and examining it would help you finally put it in place to help make the big picture—the finished puzzle? Well, in this dig you will discover lots of pieces *and* you will start connecting them!

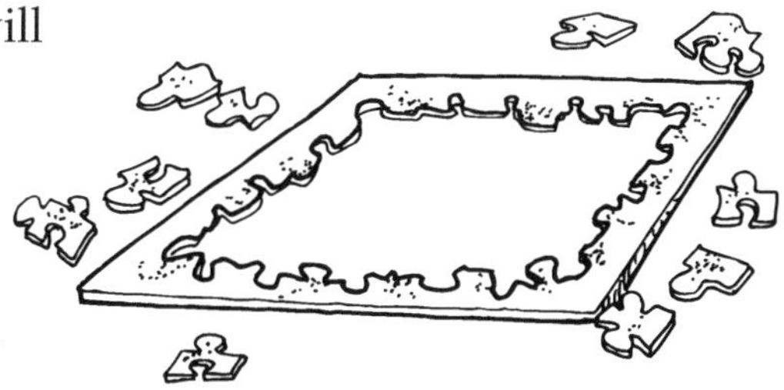

When you work on a puzzle, do you look for all the pieces with one straight side and connect them first so that you have the frame for the puzzle?

I do! I think that is the best way to begin a puzzle. Border pieces are easy to find, and it is faster to connect them. Getting that many pieces connected quickly makes you feel like you are making progress!

When you finish this dig, you still won't have the puzzle put together. But I do think you will have all the border pieces in place! Or, to say it another way, you will have the frame completed! Then, all the other truths we unearth will fit in that frame!

I am excited just talking about it, so let's dig!!!

LAYER ONE: What Is It?

The first thing we will dig out today is the definition of faith—at least it will be the definition that Hebrews 11 gives us! And the Bible's definition is the one we are interested in, right? Great, let's begin to unearth our pieces one at a time.

1. I want you to look at a verse that gives you a definition of faith. It is am amazing verse, and it will help you see the importance of digging to understand this topic.

So, read the verse below—Hebrews 11:1—and circle the word "faith."

Now faith is the assurance of things hoped for, the conviction of things not seen.
(Hebrews 1:1)

2. Next use a colored pencil to draw a squiggly line under the two things that faith is. Use the same color for both of these things. **Clue #3:** Both of these things follow the word "the," and each of the things is described using five words.

3. Do you know what the word "assurance" means? Use your dictionary to write a short definition below.

4. Now, what about the word "conviction"? Can you define it? Use your dictionary if you need to and write the definition. Keep it simple. I'm going to look this up again myself.

5. So do you have an idea about what this verse means? See if you can think it through and write what comes to your mind. Do not worry about a correct answer. We are just examining the pieces we are digging out and thinking about them, so there is no wrong answer. I will give you my idea soon.

For the moment, let me tell you my definitions just in case I got something different from you. It may help you to see someone else's work on the definitions. For the word "assurance," I wrote down this definition: certainty. That means a sure thing.

Then for the word "conviction," I wrote the definition: firm belief. That means that you believe something with all your heart and, no matter what happens to try and shake your belief, you believe anyway.

Okay, now take a minute and write your idea about what Hebrews 11:1 means.

Can you begin to see why we want to take the time to understand more about faith? Faith is what we use to believe God. It is what we use to live life the way in which God asks us! Faith can make you a person that God will call His own!

Isn't it fun to discover truth? I think it is the best! I really like knowing that I can understand the Bible myself if I will just take the time to ask the Holy Spirit to help me, to look at what it says, and to think! I know you will get more and more excited as you see the puzzle come together! See you soon in Layer Two!

LAYER TWO: Why Do I Need It?

Well, I told you that I would write out my definition of faith based on what I understood from Hebrews 11:1. So this is my idea: *Faith helps you to believe God no matter what!* What do you think? How does that compare to what you wrote?

Faith is what lets you be certain in your heart that God is going to do what He said He would do. Faith makes you sure of what you hope for and certain of what you do not see—as long as what you hope for is based on what you know God says in His Word.

Our hope can't just be something we dream up and wish for—like hoping that your parents will buy you a sporty car on your sixteenth birthday! Faith is hoping and believing that God will do something because you see it in His Word—like using all the things that happen in your life for your good. Yes, He says He wants to do that in Romans 8:28! So you can hope for and be certain that He will do that—even if you can't see how He will!

This topic of faith is really giving us lots to think about, isn't it? I like that though. It makes me feel like I am stretching my brain—just like I stretch my muscles when I hike a mountain!

So I hope you are ready to stretch today in this layer with me! There is exciting treasure in this layer for us to unearth and examine!

Today, you will discover one of the byproducts of faith. Do you know what a byproduct is? It is a funny word, but it means "a result." It is something you get for doing something—like understanding the Bible is a byproduct of taking time to study it. So today you will see a byproduct of faith, and you will be amazed, I think, to see how important faith really is!

Take a deep breath and get ready for a long, hard dig. It is going to be great, but it is going to take a while. Remember that we are building a foundation, and that takes time!

1. Look carefully at another verse from Hebrews 11 that will help you see how much you need to understand faith. Read Hebrews 11:6.

And without faith it is impossible to please *Him*, for he who comes to God must believe that He is and *that* He is a rewarder of those who seek Him. (Hebrews 11:6)

2. Go back and read the verse again and circle the word "without."

3. Now, write below what you learn about faith from the verse. Why do you need faith?

4. Yes, you have uncovered a major truth from the Word of God! Hold up this piece of the puzzle and examine it for a moment. Can you believe that you cannot please God without faith? Amazing, isn't it?

Well, if you need faith to please God, can you see why you need to understand this topic?

5. Let's continue digging in verse 6 for a few moments. Read the verse again and look closely to see what it says about someone who comes to God. The verse tells you two things that the person who comes to God should do. When you find these two things, circle each one with the same colored pencil.

6. Now, to be sure you really are examining your pieces as you discover them, I want you to take a moment longer to look at this piece. So write the two truths you just discovered about someone who comes to God. I will get you started.

He who comes to God must believe:

that _____ _____

and that He _____ ___ _____ ____ _____ _____ _____ _____

7. Do you see that to have faith—to believe even though you can't see, touch, or feel—you must accept that the Word of God is true? The Word tells us that there is a God, and Hebrews 11:6 says that we must believe that truth in order to come to God.

Let's look at another verse that tells us there is a God. It is the very first verse of the whole Bible.

In the beginning God created the heavens and the earth. (Genesis 1:1)

8. What did you learn about God?

9. So if He created the heavens and the earth, can you see that God was around before the earth and all it contains?

10. Well, what does it take to believe that God was before all of creation?

Yes, it does take faith!

11. Next, Hebrews 11:6 tells us that to come to God we must believe that God is a rewarder of the people who follow Him, who want to do what He asks them to do.

Let's look at a verse in the Old Testament that tells us this truth in another way. This verse is talking about sacrifice. The word "sacrifice" in this verse means giving up things to please God. But you will see that the Bible says there is something that is better than sacrifice.

Samuel said,
"Has the LORD as much delight in burnt offerings and sacrifices
As in obeying the voice of the LORD?
Behold, to obey is better than sacrifice,
And to heed than the fat of rams. (1 Samuel 15:22)

12. What did you see? What does the Bible say is better than sacrifice?

13. God wants you to obey! He wants you to believe Him and do what He asks you to do. Obedience is better in His eyes than giving up something *you* think may please Him.

I have a friend who gave up Saturday morning cartoons because she thought this would please her mother. Instead of watching cartoons, she slept in longer. But what would have pleased her mom was for my friend to make peanut butter and jelly sandwiches for her brothers' lunch. In fact, what her mom wanted was for my friend to watch cartoons with her younger brothers *and* make lunch!

Can you see that knowing what her mother wanted and doing it would have been better than giving up something that didn't make her mother happier? God wants us to understand what He wants us to do—and then to do it. He wants us to seek Him so that we can understand what He wants, then He wants us to obey. The reason He wants this from us is so that He can reward us!

14. So, can you see that to come to God you have to have faith? You have to believe that He is God, and you have to believe that He will reward you if you ask Him what He wants and then do it. This is what Hebrews 11:6 means when it says "a rewarder of those who seek Him"!

Both those things take faith, don't they? That is why you can't please God without faith—without it you won't believe who He is, and you won't do what He asks!

Wow! What a great piece of the puzzle you discovered in this layer of our dig! I hope you have some idea how awesome this truth is! Why don't you take a minute and thank God for giving you such an amazing opportunity? He has given you the chance to understand one of the most critical truths in His Word! And if you don't fully understand it yet, don't worry, because He will help you as you continue to do your part and dig.

I am off for a long walk—to stretch my muscles! And I want to give my brain one last long stretch, too, as I think more about this piece of the puzzle. I always like to walk when I have this kind of deep truth to think about! Care to join me?

LAYER THREE: Faith Helps to Understand

Today you are going to dig again in just one verse from Hebrews 11. This verse will help you see more of the awesome truth about faith. Can't you already see why I wanted you to dig in Hebrews with me once we started talking about faith? There are so many BIG pieces to our puzzle there! Okay, we're off!

1. Read Hebrews 11:3 below. In fact, read it two times and really think about what you are reading.

By faith we understand that the worlds were prepared by the word of God, so that what is seen was not made out of things which are visible. (Hebrews 11:3)

2. From what you just dug out, can you tell me how we can understand the creation of the world?

3. Yes, that is correct. It is only by faith that we can fully understand how the world was created! Do you know why it takes faith to believe that? Look at our verse again and see what the Bible says the world was made out of. I will help you a little.

what is seen (creation) was NOT made out of things _____ _____ _____

4. Yes, it was made out of invisible things. If we had time, we could go back and read about creation in the book of Genesis. But you can ask your mom or dad to tell you what Genesis says about creation. For now, I will just remind you that God spoke—just like Hebrews 11:3 says—and things were created! So, the things we see every day were not created from things that were seen!
In other words, God did not take two trees and mix them together to make a third tree. There were *no* trees! God spoke, and trees were made. That is incredible!
But now to the point! This verse tells us plainly that it is only by faith that we can believe the Bible's creation story. Other people may give you different stories about creation, but the only true account is in God's Word. And it takes faith to believe it!
Now, think about what you have uncovered in this layer. Okay, write out below, in your own words, why faith is so important—using only what you have discovered in this layer, not in any of the others and not in the last dig.

Can you see how basic faith is? You need it to believe that God is God. You need it to believe that He will reward you if you follow His way. You need it to believe that He created the world and all mankind!

Faith surely is a major part of our Christian life, isn't it?
Take a moment right now and ask God to help you really understand this topic.

LAYER FOUR: Faith = Approval

Today's dig will not be as hard as some of the others you have just completed. I am extrememly proud of your diligence, and I am very happy that you have a desire to understand faith! You are doing well, and today you will be rewarded for your hard work with a layer that is easier to dig through.

We are going to look again in Hebrews 11 to see what else we can uncover about faith. Again, we will look only at one verse, and it is a very short one!

1. Read Hebrews 11:2.

For by it the men of old gained approval. (Hebrews 11:2)

2. Your first question may be about what the word "it." What is the "it" in this verse? That is a very, very good question. If you asked the question, I am impressed because you are paying very close attention as you examine your pieces.

If I had written out verses 1 and 2 for you, you would have seen that the word "it" refers to the word "faith" from the first verse. So, in verse 2, the word "it" means faith. Go back now and read verse 2 and use the word "faith" as you read instead of the word "it."

3. What did you discover? Think and write what you learn about faith.

4. Whose approval do you think the men of old gained? Think back to Layer One. Whom does faith please?

5. That's right. It pleases God. So whose approval did these men of old gain by their faith?

6. Why don't you take a few minutes and work the fun puzzle on page 33. I think you will have a great time with it!

Very good! You have another interesting piece of the puzzle! Think about it, and rest up because Layer Five will be a longer dig than this one! And I know you will want to be ready and rarin' to go! See you then.

LAYER FIVE: The Faith Hall of Fame

Well, here we are again! I have been thinking about you because when you reached the bottom of Layer Four you discovered that "men of old" gained approval through faith. Perhaps you have been wondering who these people were and what their faith may have lead them to do as they followed God.

Well, even if you haven't been wondering, I have been thinking about it and hoping that together we can dig out truths today that will help you understand these things.

I am more than ready to go, and I hope you are, too.

1. Some people call Hebrews 11 the faith hall of fame because God names men and women who lived by faith—men and women who did what He asked them to do.

You may have heard some of the stories about these men and women. I bet you know about Abraham, Moses, King David, and Noah. You probably have heard some of the other names, but you may not know the story of their faith, like Abel, Gideon, Rahab, and Jacob.

Exciting news! We are going to dig through stories about these men and women so we can see the kind of faith that God rewards. We will look at the lives of the people God calls men and women of faith!

But before we begin to look at each of their stories, let's see if we can understand more about the faith they had and what God promised them.

2. There are a few verses that tell us God made a promise to these men and women and that the promise was fulfilled.

Read Hebrews 11:32-34 below and discover what it says about the promise. You really only need to read verse 33 to dig up this treasure, but the other two verses are so exciting that I knew you would want to read them, too!

³²And what more shall I say? For time will fail me if I tell of Gideon, Barak, Samson, Jephthah, of David and Samuel and the prophets, ³³who by faith conquered kingdoms, performed *acts of* righteousness, obtained promises, shut the mouths of lions, ³⁴quenched the power of fire, escaped the edge of the sword, from weakness were made strong, became mighty in war, put foreign armies to flight.

(Hebrews 11:32-34)

3. What did you see about these men when it comes to promises?

4. Yes, they obtained them! This, of course, means that God promised them something and they got what He promised—all because the men had faith in God, that He would do what He said, and because they followed Him. Awesome, right?

5. But there is a bit of a twist to our study! We are going to look now at other verses in the Bible that tell us God also made a promise to these men and women that they never saw happen! Let's look at some verses in Hebrews that talk about the promise that did not happen—and about why it did not happen.

I realize this part of the dig is a little rough! It is hard digging, for sure. But what you are about to uncover will make the hard work extremely worthwhile!

Read Hebrews 11:39-40 below and see what you can learn about what was promised this time.

> ³⁹And all these, having gained approval through their faith, did not receive what was promised, ⁴⁰because God had provided something better for us, so that apart from us they would not be made perfect. (Hebrews 11:39-40)

6. Write what you discovered about what was promised.

7. Now, read the verses again and see why these men and women did not receive this promise. There are really two reasons, so let me help you to be sure you get both.

  because God had provided something _____ _____ _____

  so that apart from us they would not be made _____

8. Are you surprised to see that the reason the promise was not fulfilled had something to do with us. Yes, that means with you, too! Can you imagine what it is? Let's find out.

> ¹⁴The Lord God said to the serpent,
> "Because you have done this,
> Cursed are you more than all cattle,
> And more than every beast of the field;
> On your belly you will go,
> And dust you will eat
> All the days of your life;

¹⁵"And I will put enmity
Between you and the woman,
And between your seed and her seed;
He shall bruise you on the head,
And you shall bruise him on the heel." (Genesis 3:14-15)

9. Do you remember that the serpent tempted Eve and told her she could eat a fruit that God had told her not to eat? Eve believed his lie and ate the fruit. She then gave the fruit to Adam, and he ate it too.

When Eve and Adam sinned, God cursed the serpent and said that there would be enmity (that means "trouble") between him and the children of the woman (that's us). Then God promised that He would send someone to save them from sin. In these verses, He says He will send someone to crush the head of the serpent. He also says that the serpent will bruise that man on the heel. Do you know how Jesus died? Yes, He was crucified! And when a man is crucified, his hands and his heels are nailed to a cross. So Jesus' heels were bruised. Yes, Jesus is the man who will come to crush the serpent and save us from sin!

God made the promise in words that you may have a hard time understanding, so read the verses above again and let me try to help you.

10. All the men and women in Hebrews 11 who walked with God knew this promise. God had said He was going to send a man who would save people from sin, and these people believed it. Think hard now. Did any of these people live long enough to see Jesus?

11. You are correct. They were all dead when Jesus came to the earth. But they did believe that Jesus was coming! They had the faith to look forward to that day.

Think back now to the verses from Hebrews 11 about the promise they did not receive. It talks of a promise God made to us. Well, God promised us, too, that we could be saved from our sin.

How are you saved from sin? You look back on what happened when Jesus came to earth and died, and *by faith* (there is our word again) you believe He died for you!

So, can you think of why the promise God made to us would be called "better" than the one He made to them? You will have to think very, very hard, but I think you may get it.

I think our promise is better because, even though we have to believe by faith that Jesus died, we can look back and believe something that is recorded in history. It *did* happen.

For the men and women of Hebrews 11 to have faith in Jesus, they had to look forward to something that was going to happen. There was no record of the event. They had to believe that it *would* happen!

You and I can read in the Bible about eyewitness accounts of the death of Jesus. These men and women had to believe without anyone ever seeing Jesus' death!

So, you see that these men and women of faith had some promises fulfilled in their lives, but they never saw God fulfill the promise of what He would do for them and for all people. However, because they believed God and trusted that He would one day do what He said, they all lived lives of faith. They were such great men and women of faith that God recorded them in His Word so that one day you and I could read about their faith!

Don't you want to be the kind of guy or gal of faith that God would be proud to call His! I bet you do! And in these next nine digs, we are going to look more closely at the lives of some of these men and women so we can understand more about faith—and so we can become people of faith!

You have just come to the bottom of an awesome, amazing dig. Record your "Truth Treasures" and then take a well-deserved break and consider all the treasure you have uncovered—all those pieces of the puzzle you can add to the ones on the table!

I hope you will take time to do something fun since I know you have earned it. And I will see you in Dig Three—soon, I hope!

Truth Treasures for the Week

1.

2.

3.

Bury the Treasure:

And without fatih, it is impossible to please Him, for he who comes to God must believe that He is and that He is a rewarder of those who seek Him. (Hebrews 11:6)

The Power of Faith

Missing Pieces Puzzle

You're learning a lot of big words and big ideas in this dig! Let's play a game to help you remember them. First, use the missing letters listed below to fill in the blanks in the crossword puzzle. It might help you to cross out each letter as you go. After you fill in each blank in numbers 1-17, transfer those letters to the corresponding numbered squares in the diagram to discover the key to the power of faith.

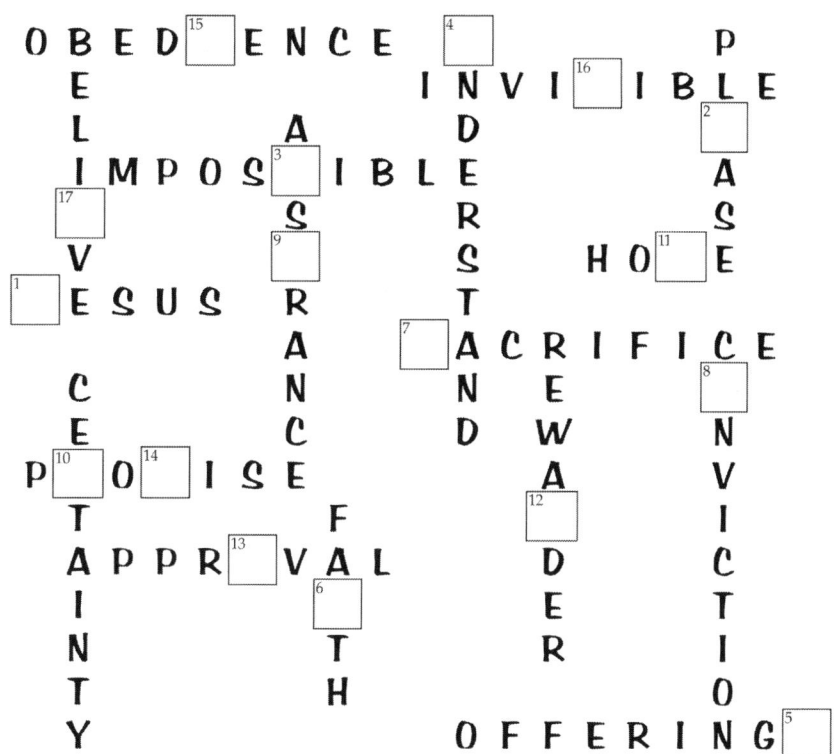

solution on page 163

Dig 3

Abel and the Obedience of Faith

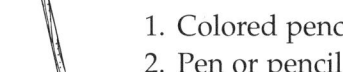

Tools of the Trade

1. Colored pencils
2. Pen or pencil
3. Game on page 45

Directions for Diggers

I am writing this dig for you just a few days after the World Trade Center attack of September 11, 2001. And as I think about the men and women you are going to study now, it makes me think of the many men and women who died on September 11.

Why? Because the men and women of Hebrews 11 are heroes of faith, and many of the men and women who died on September 11 saved others before their own deaths. They became heroes to our nation.

In particular, I think of the people on United Flight 93 that crashed in Pennsylvania. Several young men on that flight decided to try and stop the attack that the terrorists on the plane were planning.

Think back about how much you've heard about these young men—of their bravery, of their heroism, of their determination to stop what they believed would be another attack on our nation's capitol. And think of all the lives they saved in the process!

You may remember that, as President Bush spoke to Congress after the attack, the wife of a young man who died on Flight 93 was in the audience. The president honored Lisa Beamer's husband, Todd, by asking her to stand, so all the world could see her and think about what her husband and the others on Flight 93 had done.

The kind of honor that President Bush placed on Todd Beamer and others is the kind of honor that God places on the men and women of Hebrews 11. He recorded their names in His Word so that all the generations to come could think about how these men and women lived. God wanted us to know that these were men and women who lived by faith.

I am very excited to be at this point in our dig! We are to the best part, I think, because we can start digging out truths about men and women—people just like us—that will help us understand how to live our lives *by faith*!

So let's dig and see what we can discover about faith by looking at the life of Abel.

LAYER ONE: Who Is Abel?

As you gather up your tools and get ready to dig, don't forget to check in with headquarters! And when you check in today, ask God to show you truths that will help you become a guy or gal of faith—a person that God would be proud to call His own, someone that He would ask to stand to honor the way you live by faith!

Okay, are you ready? Me, too! Let's do it!

1. Read Hebrews 11:4 and find out what is said about the hero whose faith you will learn about in this dig.

> By faith Abel offered to God a better sacrifice than Cain, through which he obtained the testimony that he was righteous, god testifying about his gifts and through faith, though he is dead, he still speaks. (Hebrews 11:4)

2. If you think hard, I bet you can remember some of the story about Abel. But, if you are like me, you can't remember the entire story. So let's take some time to dig around in Genesis and sift through the story about Abel.

As you dig, whenever you see Abel's name, use your colored pencil—your blue one—and circle his name.

¹Now the man had relations with his wife Eve, and she conceived and gave birth to Cain, and she said, "I have gotten a manchild with *the help of* the LORD." ²Again, she gave birth to his brother Abel. And Abel was a keeper of flocks, but Cain was a tiller of the ground. ³So it came about in the course of time that Cain brought an offering to the

Abel and the Obedience of Faith

LORD of the fruit of the ground. ⁴Abel, on his part also brought of the firstlings of his flock and of their fat portions. And the LORD had regard for Abel and for his offering; ⁵but for Cain and for his offering He had no regard. So Cain became very angry and his countenance fell. ⁶Then the LORD said to Cain, "Why are you angry? And why has your countenance fallen? ⁷"If you do well, will not *your countenance* be lifted up? And if you do not do well, sin is crouching at the door; and its desire is for you, but you must master it." ⁸Cain told Abel his brother. And it came about when they were in the field, that Cain rose up against Abel his brother and killed him. (Genesis 4:1-8)

Let's examine what you just uncovered by thinking through some questions.

3. Who are Abel's parents?

4. Who is Abel's brother?

5. What was Abel's job?

6. What was Cain's job?

Great! You have begun to dig out truth about Abel that will help you understand why God calls him a man of faith. And you have gathered truth that will help you become a guy or gal of faith, too. You will see how in the layers to come!

LAYER TWO: Where Are You?

As we head off to dig for more truths that will help you understand Abel's faith—and why God notes him in Hebrews 11—don't forget to check in with headquarters.

1. As we begin to dig in Layer Two, we are going back a little further in the book of Genesis to examine some verses that talk about Abel's parents. But before you begin to dig in Genesis 3:8-12, let me catch you up on what has happened earlier in Genesis.

You remember, I am sure, that God made man and woman then put them in a beautiful garden to live. He told them that they could eat the fruit from all the trees in the garden except one, and He explained to them why they could not eat from it.

But then the serpent, Satan, talks with Eve and tells her that God has lied to her. Satan says that the fruit of the tree is good to eat and that it will not kill her like God said. So, Eve eats and lives. She then gives the fruit to her husband Adam. Adam eats the fruit—and he doesn't die either!

Here is the tricky part: God did not mean that Adam and Eve would *physically* die if they ate the fruit—He did not mean their bodies would die at that moment. God was telling Eve that they would *spiritually* die at that moment they ate the fruit. Their disobedience would separate them from God, and they would no longer walk and talk with Him in the garden.

God made man and woman to have a friendship with Him, and He knew if they disobeyed Him and ate the fruit that this friendship would be ruined—that they would die spiritually and would feel afraid before Him.

After Adam and Eve eat the fruit, God is in the garden. God knows what has happened. Let's dig through the story and see what we uncover!

⁸They heard the sound of the LORD God walking in the garden in the cool of the day, and the man and his wife hid themselves from the presence of the LORD God among the trees of the garden. ⁹Then the LORD God called to the man, and said to him, "Where are you?" ¹⁰He said, "I heard the sound of You in the garden, and I was afraid because I was naked; so I hid myself." ¹¹And He said, "Who told you that you were naked? Have you eaten from the tree of which I commanded you not to eat?" ¹²The man said, "The woman whom You gave *to be* with me, she gave me from the tree, and I ate." (Genesis 3:8-12)

2. What do Adam and Eve do when they hear God in the garden?

3. In verse 10, Adam tells God why they hid. What does he say made them hide?

4. God asks Adam two questions in response to what he says. Look in verse 11 and write the first question God asks below.

5. What else does God say in verse 11? Write out God's second question.

God knew, didn't He? Yes, He knew that Adam and Eve had disobeyed Him. How did God know? Think about why Adam said they were hiding. Yes, he said they hid because they were naked. When Adam gave this reason for hiding, God knew what had happened.

Adam and Eve had been naked since God created them, but they had never been ashamed to be naked before! Now that they had sinned—by doing what God told them not to do—they were ashamed. And they showed their shame by hiding from God.

6. After God talks with everyone involved in the sin, He does something for Adam and Eve to help them with their shame. Let's see what it is. Read Genesis 3:21.

> The LORD God made garments of skin for Adam and his wife, and clothed them.
> (Genesis 3:21)

Yes, God made garments so that they could cover their bodies. We are going to talk more in Layer Three about the garments that God made for Adam and Eve. Today you have done a great job digging through Genesis.

It may be hard to see how this layer of digging will help in understanding Abel's faith. But, remember, we are digging out pieces and fitting them together! And although it may be hard to see how the pieces you uncovered today will fit with what we are digging out about Abel's faith, they will!

Take a break and have some cookies and milk since you have been digging so hard for the last few minutes!

LAYER THREE: Sin Covered

I hope you are ready for an exciting day! I think you will be jazzed about what you are going to uncover today.

In Layer Two we discovered that Adam and Eve hid after they had sinned. And because God knew they were ashamed, He made garments for them to wear. I bet you are wondering about these garments, aren't you? I hope you are, because that means you are thinking!

Well, I am excited to dig with you today and uncover truths that will answer your questions about the garments. So, let's dig!

1. Let's dig again in a verse you started to dig in yesterday. When you dig today, see if you can uncover the answer to this question: What kind of garments did God make for Adam and Eve?

> The LORD God made garments of skin for Adam and his wife, and clothed them.
> (Genesis 3:21)

2. If God made garments of skin, what kind of skin do you think He used?

3. Yes, I think God used the skin of an animal to make garments for Adam and Eve. I don't know what kind of an animal He used, but I know He used an animal skin for the garments.

Let's look at a verse in Hebrews that will help you understand why God made the coverings from animal skin. As you work through this verse, take your red pencil and circle three words: "without," "shedding," and "no."

> ¹⁹For when every commandment had been spoken by Moses to all the people according to the Law, he took the blood of the calves and the goats, with water and scarlet wool and hyssop, and sprinkled both the book itself and all the people, ²⁰saying, "This is the blood of the covenant which God commanded you." ²¹And in the same way he sprinkled both the tabernacle and all the vessels of the ministry with the blood. ²²And according to the Law, *one may* almost *say*, all things are cleansed with blood, and without shedding of blood there is no forgiveness.
> (Hebrews 9:19-22)

4. There is a truth in these verses that is important for you to learn if you are going to understand Abel's faith. So let's slow down and carefully look at it.

You circled three words that should help you uncover this truth. If you look carefully at the words you circled, you will discover that something had to happen for Adam and Eve's sin to be forgiven or covered. Look back at the verse and the words you circled, and write below what was necessary for forgiveness.

5. Remember that God had a plan to cover man's sin once and for all? That's right, Jesus was going to die for man's sin. But it was not time for that BIG PLAN yet. So, God put another plan in place to cover sin and forgive man until the Big Plan was ready to unfold.

So, God said that—until it was time for the Big Plan—He would allow man's sin to be covered by the shedding of the blood of an animal. And the first time that man's sin was covered in this way in the story of Adam and Eve!

God had to kill an animal to make the skins to cover Adam and Eve, and the animal's blood was shed when God killed it for its skin. The animal's blood covered their sin, and its skin covered their nakedness and shame.

Now, whether you realize it or not, you have the pieces of the puzzle that will help you fully understand Abel's faith! So in Layer Four, we will see how Abel pleased God and became a hero of faith!

6. Since you have had a shorter dig today, why don't you have some fun with the puzzle on page 45?

I know it must be hard to dig and dig and not yet be able to put the truths you have uncovered together to see the big picture, but remember that gathering truths—pieces of the puzzle—is all a part of studying the Word of God. Hang in there, you will start connecting pieces soon!

Have a good rest of the day, and do something fun. I am going to enjoy one of my favorite things this afternoon! And I will see you in Layer Four soon!

LAYER FOUR: Abel's Offering

I am excited that today you can connect the truths you have uncovered to really understand Abel's faith! I hope you are eager to get started because I am. Let's dig!

1. Let's go back and look at the story of Abel again so that it is fresh in your mind. Then we can talk about his faith. Go back to Layer One (pages 36-37) and read Genesis 4:1-8 again in number 2.

2. What kind of an offering did Abel offer to God?

3. What did you discover in Layer Three about the kind of offering that God required to cover sin?

That's right. God required an animal offering.

4. What did Cain offer to God? Look back in verse 3 if you need to be reminded.

5. What does the last part of verse 4 say about the way God felt about Abel's offering?

6. What does verse 5 say about how God felt toward Cain's offering?

7. What did Cain do for a living? Look in verse 2.

8. What did Abel do to make his living?

9. Abel was keeping flocks, so he had an animal! Do you think it is fair to ask Cain to sacrifice an animal when he was a farmer?

God had said what He required to cover sin—an animal sacrifice. So, even though Cain was a farmer, he could have traded some of his grain for an animal, couldn't he?

10. Let's look at a verse in another book of the Bible that tells us how God felt about Cain's offering. You will discover in this verse what happened to Cain and Abel, too.

not as Cain, *who* was of the evil one and slew his brother. And for what reason did he slay him? Because his deeds were evil, and his brother's were righteous. (1 John 3:12)

11. You see, don't you, that in the end he was so upset that Abel had obeyed and gained God's approval that Cain killed Abel? What does the verse above tell you about Cain's actions? Read carefully. The verse is talking about the offering Cain made when it talks about his actions. It is not talking about the fact that he killed Abel.

Of course, the murder was evil, too. But we all know murder is evil. I want to be sure you see what the verse is saying: The offering Cain made was evil—evil because he did not obey what God had said about the kind of offering he should make.

Abel had the faith to obey what God asked—even if he did not fully understand it. Obviously, his brother did not think the *kind* of offering was important. Cain just thought it was an offering that mattered. But Abel obeyed. In obedient faith, he offered what God asked.

You've dug hard, and I am proud of you! See if you can share what you have discovered today with your mom or dad. Talk with them about Abel's sacrifice and why you think he made the correct choice in what he offered. Also talk about why Cain's choice was the wrong one.

I will be looking forward to seeing you in Layer Five!

LAYER FIVE: The Importance of Obedience

When we got to the bottom of Layer Four you discovered that Abel's faith shows the importance of obedience. You discovered by looking at the story of Cain and Abel that, when we know what God says, we must obey—even if others do not.

Abel and the Obedience of Faith

1. Let's dig through another verse in the Old Testament that talks about how important obedience is to the Lord. We've dug in this verse before. I bet you'll remember it.

Underline with your green pencil the words "obey" and "obeying" when you come to them.

Samuel said,
"Has the LORD as much delight in burnt offerings and sacrifices
As in obeying the voice of the LORD?
Behold, to obey is better than sacrifice,
And to heed than the fat of rams. (1 Samuel 15:22)

OBEDIENCE

2. The prophet Samuel is talking to King Saul in the verse you just read. Saul had done something that God had told him not to do. What does Samuel tell Saul that obedience is better than? Write your answer below.

3. Yes, Samuel says that it is better to obey God than to offer sacrifice. You discovered in Layer Four how important sacrifice was to God. And you saw, too, how critical it was to offer the sacrifice He asked.

But here you see that the true key is obedience! And if you think back to the story of Cain and Abel, you will see that even in that story the key was obedience. Abel obeyed God and offered an animal sacrifice, and Cain disobeyed and offered grain.

So, in the story of Cain and Abel, you learn that it was obedience that made the difference. Both Cain and Abel made an offering, but only one of them offered what God asked. It was not the offering that was important—it was the kind of offering. It was obeying God that truly mattered.

So, what is the key to pleasing God? Read the verse above again and write below what Samuel says is better than sacrifice.

Can you understand that Abel was a man of faith because he obeyed God? He did not let his brother's behavior affect him. He may not have been able to understand why he needed to offer an animal; he simply did what God had asked him to do.

4. Now that you've sketched about the truth of this dig, record in words three "Truth Treasures."

Will you be a guy or a girl who lives in obedience by faith? Remember, when you know what God wants you to do, you should do it no matter what all of your friends do or say! The way to please God is to walk in obedience by faith!

Truth Treasures for the Week

1.

2.

3.

Bury the Treasure:

Does the Lord delight in burnt offerings and sacrifices as much as in obeying the voice of the Lord? To obey is better than sacrifice, and to heed is better than the fat of rams.

(1 Samuel 15:22)

Abel and the Obedience of Faith

Maze Puzzler

Find your way through the maze! When you've made it to the finish, circle the letters that your pencil passed through on the way, then unscramble them to uncover one of the truths from your dig. Watch out for dead ends and wrong turns! These extra letters will try to lead you astray.

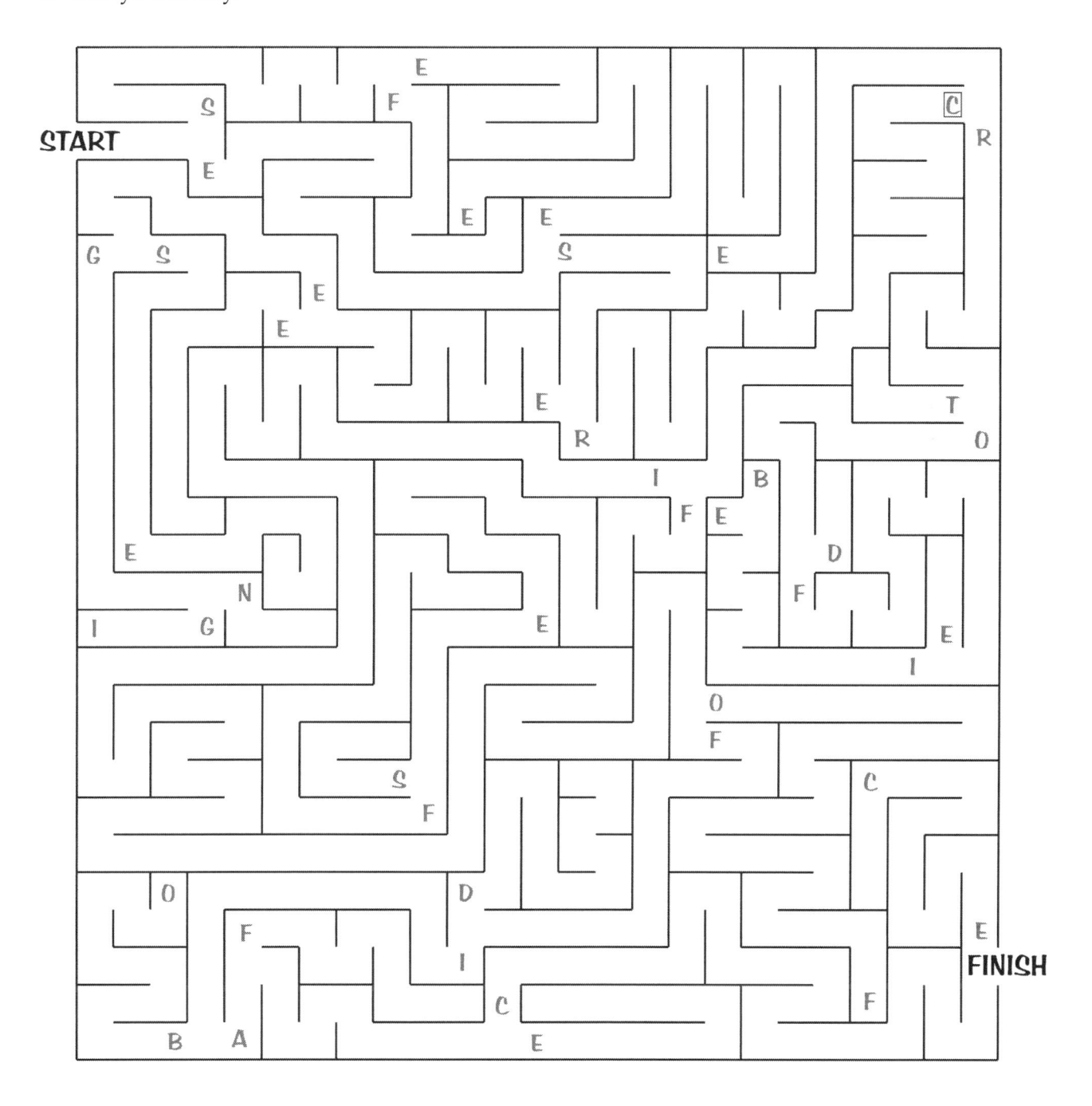

To obey is better than...

___ ___ ___ ___ ___ ___ ___ ___ ___

solution on page 164

Dig 4

Enoch and the Devotion of Faith

Tools of the Trade

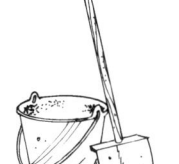

1. Colored pencils
2. Pen or pencil
3. Dictionary
4. Game on page 55

Directions for Diggers

The man whose faith we will examine in this dig is Enoch. Maybe you have never even heard of Enoch since there is not a lot recorded about him in the Bible. But I bet you have heard of his grandson, Noah!

You may wonder why we would take the time to dig through the story of a man who has so little written about him in the Bible. Well, think with me for a moment. Remember, he is one of the heroes of faith named in Hebrews 11, so that alone should get our attention and tell us that there is something about his faith we need to understand.

You will also see two very important facts in the few verses that talk about him. In these two facts, you will find a treasure about the kind of faith Enoch had, and you will learn something from this treasure about the kind of faith we are supposed to have!

So, let's begin our dig on the faith of Enoch. Remember to check in with headquarters.

Truth Trackers: Heroes of Faith

LAYER ONE: Walking Before God!

I am ready to dig, are you? Great! Let's get going!

1. Begin by reading what the Bible records about Enoch in Genesis 5:21-24.

²¹Enoch lived sixty-five years, and became the father of Methuselah. ²²Then Enoch walked with God three hundred years after he became the father of Methuselah, and he had *other* sons and daughters. ²³So all the days of Enoch were three hundred and sixty-five years. ²⁴Enoch walked with God; and he was not, for God took him.
(Genesis 5:21-24)

2. When Enoch was sixty-five years old he had a son and named him Methuselah. What does verse 22 say that Enoch did after this son was born?

3. How long did Enoch walk with God?

People sure lived a lot longer then than they do now, didn't they!

4. So, this is the entire story of the man whose faith you are digging to understand. When you think of how big the Bible is, it is hard to believe that this is the whole story about him, isn't it? Well, I hope you are wondering why Enoch is one of the heroes listed in Hebrews 11. I want you to really think about his faith and what there was about it that caused God to list him. And as you think, answer this question again: What does verse 24 say Enoch did?

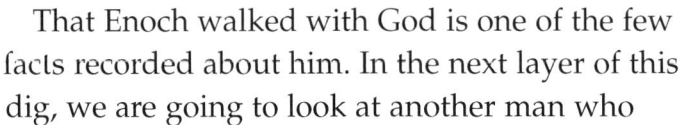

That Enoch walked with God is one of the few facts recorded about him. In the next layer of this dig, we are going to look at another man who walked before God and see what we can learn about what it may mean to walk with or before God.

Think about what it could mean to walk with God and meet me in Layer Two as soon as you can. I can hardly wait to show you what I want you to see.

I hope you can take a nice break now. I think I will watch one of my favorite videos

and have one of my favorite snacks—popcorn and hot apple cider! Maybe you can watch one of your favorite videos and
have a great snack too! See you soon!

LAYER TWO: Hezekiah, Too!

I am so glad you are back and ready to go. I have been eager to dig more and see what we can find about walking with God. Have you been thinking about what it might mean? I sure have! Let's dig in and see what you uncover.

1. You are going to read about another man of the Old Testament who was a king. His name is Hezekiah. In the section of Scripture we are going to read, Hezekiah is sick. Read 2 Kings 20:1-6 and see what you learn about this man.

> ¹In those days Hezekiah became mortally ill. And Isaiah the prophet the son of Amoz came to him and said to him, "Thus says the LORD, 'Set your house in order, for you shall die and not live.'" ²Then he turned his face to the wall, and prayed to the LORD, saying, ³"Remember now, O LORD, I beseech You, how I have walked before You in truth and with a whole heart and have done what is good in Your sight." And Hezekiah wept bitterly. ⁴Before Isaiah had gone out of the middle court, the word of the LORD came to him, saying, ⁵"Return and say to Hezekiah the leader of My people, 'Thus says the LORD, the God of your father David, "I have heard your prayer, I have seen your tears; behold, I will heal you. On the third day you shall go up to the house of the LORD. ⁶"I will add fifteen years to your life, and I will deliver you and this city from the hand of the king of Assyria; and I will defend this city for My own sake and for My servant David's sake."'" (2 Kings 20:1-6)

2. Verse 1 says Hezekiah was "mortally" ill. This means that he was dying. What was the message God sent to him in verse 1? Write it below.

3. What did Hezekiah do when he got the message? Look in verse 2.

4. Hezekiah reminds God of how he has lived his life. What does he say to God? I'll help you a little. Look in verse 3 and fill in the things he said to God below.

I have _____ _____ _____ ____ _____

and with a _____ _____

and have done what _____ _____ _____ _____ _____

5. Read verses 4-6 again. Did God hear the prayer we see recorded in verse 3?

6. What did God do for Hezekiah? God says what He will do about his illness in verse 5.

Yes, God healed him and told him he would live for fifteen more years.

Men who walk with God or before God and obey Him have faith in Him. They believe what He says and do what He asks. And you can see that the fact that Hezekiah had walked before God and served Him with a whole heart made a difference! God listened and answered his prayer!

LAYER THREE: Walk How?

Hey, you are back already! Great! The digging in each layer of this dig hasn't been too hard, has it? Well, today's dig is not too deep either, but I am ready to get started and excited about the verses we will dig in. So, let's go!

1. Micah was a prophet. A prophet was someone who heard a message from God and spoke it to the people with whom God wanted to communicate. Micah spoke to the people who lived in Samaria and Jerusalem. So, he was talking to God's people.

Read the verses below from the book of Micah and see what you can find about walking before God.

> ⁷Does the LORD take delight in thousands of rams,
> In ten thousand rivers of oil?
> Shall I present my firstborn *for* my rebellious acts,
> The fruit of my body for the sin of my soul?
> ⁸He has told you, O man, what is good;
> And what does the LORD require of you
> But to do justice, to love kindness,
> And to walk humbly with your God? (Micah 6:7-8)

2. Can you see that God does not so much delight in sacrifices the people make as He delights in their walking before Him—in the way in which He asks them? Read verse 7 and then look at the first sentence of verse 8.

Enoch and the Devotion of Faith

Micah talks about the sacrifices, but then he says God has told the people what is good and what He requires. Then you see the list of things God wants the people to do. Look at verse 8 again, and write down what God requires them to do.

- to

- to

- to

3. What is the last thing on the list? Write it again.

4. What does it mean to walk humbly before God? Well, guess what you need to do to help see what it means. Look up the word "humble" in your dictionary and write the definition below.

God wants these people—and you—to walk before Him in a way that shows you want to do what He asks you to do. We should always want to do the right thing because it is the thing that will please God. We should obey in a way that does not fight what God asks and in a way that is devoted to doing what *God* wants you to do—not what you think is best or what everyone else is doing.

5. Do you want to walk humbly before God? Write down your thoughts about how you want to walk with God.

6. Do these verses remind you of another verse you have dug into? Think back to Dig Three. It is even the verse you hid in your heart! Write the reference here.

Truth Trackers: Heroes of Faith

You have done a good day of digging.
Put up your tools and take a nice break.
I will look forward to seeing you in
Layer Four!

LAYER FOUR: Enoch Got "Took"!

I am sure you see now—from Hezekiah's story and from the verses out of the book of Micah—that a very important part of walking and talking with God is being willing to do what He asks!

Two other men in the faith hall of fame are Abraham and Moses, and you will dig through their stories, too. When you do, you will see that sometimes it can be hard to believe when you can't see how something will happen, but that is what faith is all about—walking with God and obeying anyway!

1. Now, let's go back to the man whose faith we are looking at in this dig: Read Hebrews 11:5 two times and think hard as you read.

> By faith Enoch was taken up so that he would not see death; and he was not found because God took him up; for he obtained the witness that before his being taken up he was pleasing to God. (Hebrews 11:5)

2. Write below what you learn about Enoch in the verse above. I will get you started on each truth you should note.

Enoch was taken up so that he _____ _____ _____ _____

He was not found because _____ _____ _____ _____

He obtained the witness that before his being taken up he was _____ _____ _____

3. Read Enoch's story again. Look back to Layer One and read Genesis 5:21-24. Read carefully and look for what else you can learn in verse 24 about this man named Enoch, besides the fact that he walked with God. You just saw it, too, in Hebrews 11! Record what you see below.

4. What does the Bible mean when it says that "he was not, for God took him"? Think about it and write your thoughts below.

You are right! It means that Enoch was here on the earth one moment and the next moment he was gone! God took him! He did not die! Enoch was just caught up in the sky to heaven. When I think of how that must have happened, I think of how the wind catches a kite and pulls it up into the sky. I think God reached down and scooped Enoch up like the wind catches a kite, but God took Enoch all the way up to be with Him!

Can you imagine what it would be like to be here with your friends one second then suddenly be headed up to be with God the next—and still be alive in your body? Awesome!

Well, Enoch not only walked with God, he pleased God as well. And when God was ready to have Enoch come be with Him, He just took him!

LAYER FIVE: God Was Pleased!

Okay, it is hard to believe that we are almost to the bottom of this dig, but we are getting there in a hurry! As we start digging today, I hope your question is: What was so special about Enoch's faith? What kind of faith did he have that pleased God?

1. Think back to the work you did in Layer Two and Layer Three. What did you learn about what kind of heart you need to have if you are going to walk with God?

Yes, those who walk and talk with God need to be willing to do all that God asks. So, if this is part of walking with God, don't you think that it would be true of Enoch, too? Don't you think Enoch did all that God asked him to do?

2. Think about the fact that the Bible says God was *pleased* with Enoch. Wouldn't you be excited to think that God could record that about you? When I think of the kind of faith that Enoch had—the kind of faith that would cause God to say He was pleased—a certain word comes to my mind. I think of the word "devotion." Grab your dictionary and look up the word. Write down what you find.

3. My dictionary gave me this definition: enthusiastic attachment or loyalty to a person or cause; a great love.

I think Enoch had a devoted faith. I think he totally loved God and was totally loyal to Him. I do not think Enoch wondered if he should do what God asked. I think he did all that God asked enthusiastically. I think it is this kind of faith that pleased God. I believe it is this kind of faith that resulted in Enoch's being "took." God was so pleased with Enoch's faith that Enoch did not die, God just took him! Amazing!

4. Do you want to have this kind of faith? Do you want to be loyal to God? Do you want to obey enthusiastically no matter what God asks you to do? Write out your thoughts.

I pray that you will have a great love for God that results in devoted faith. And I think you are on the right track by taking time to dig in the Word of God. Knowing the Word will help you know what God wants you to do! Spending time in the Word of God will help you get to know God, too—and the more you know Him, the more you will want to serve Him loyally!

5. Take a moment now and see if you can solve the puzzle on page 55 before you head off for more fun with your friends.

6. Don't forget your "Truth Treasures."

As you work through these truths about the men and women of faith you are studying in the next eight digs, ask God to show you how you to live in such a way that your faith will become as strong as theirs was!

I am proud of you for digging all the way through this layer. See you in Dig Five!

Truth Treasures for the Week

1.

2.

3.

Bury the Treasure:

He has told you, O man, what is good. And what does the Lord require of you but to do justice, to love kindness, and to walk humbly with your God? (Micah 6:8)

Enoch and the Devotion of Faith

Hidden Truths

We learned about three important people in this dig. Here is a game to help you remember these men who each had a special kind of faith. Follow the instructions below.

1) Go through each line of type below and cross out the following letters:

   B J Q U X

   Go through once and cross out the Bs. Then go back and cross out the Js. Then the Qs, the Us, and finally the Xs.
2) Now look at the letters left in number one and see what words you can form from the remaining letters. Write what you see, and discover a truth from our dig.
3) Do the same to number 2 and 3.

The Devotion of Faith

1. B E J N X O C Q H U W B A L Q K J E D U W B I T U H G X O U D B

   Hidden Truth: _____

2. U H B E Q Z J E U K Q I J A B H X P Q R B J A X Y U E B D Q
   A J N U D W J A Q S X H B E U A J L Q E X D U J

   Hidden Truth: _____

3. J M Q I B C X A B H X S P U O K Q E J T U O X T B H E Q U P E X O
   J U U P Q L X E B O J F Q G B O X D U

   Hidden Truth: _____

solution on page 164

Dig 5

Noah and a Trusting Faith

Tools of the Trade

1. Colored pencils
2. Pen or pencil
3. Dictionary
4. Game on page 68

Directions for Diggers

I hope you are ready for another exciting dig! I am still thinking about the man we talked about last dig, Enoch. It is amazing to me that Enoch's faith was so strong and devoted that God just took him!

In the dig we are gearing up for today, guess whose faith we are going to examine? I bet you can't guess, so I'll tell you. It is someone I think you know a lot about already—Noah. Do you remember that I mentioned in the last dig that Enoch was Noah's grandfather? Interesting, isn't it?

As you gather up your tools to head out with me, think about the fact that Noah is listed in Hebrews 11 because of his faith and that his grandfather Enoch is also listed because of his faith. It makes me wonder if Noah learned about trusting God by watching how his grandfather lived!

Well, I've got all my stuff together. Do you? Great! Let's head off.

LAYER ONE: A Sad World

1. As we begin our dig, let's read the story of Noah. It may take us a couple of layers to work our way through the whole story, but it is such a great story I know you won't even think about the length.

> ⁵Then the LORD saw that the wickedness of man was great on the earth, and that every intent of the thoughts of his heart was only evil continually. ⁶The LORD was sorry that He had made man on the earth, and He was grieved in His heart. ⁷The LORD said, "I will blot out man whom I have created from the face of the land, from man to animals to creeping things and to birds of the sky; for I am sorry that I have made them." ⁸But Noah found favor in the eyes of the LORD.
>
> ⁹These are *the records of* the generations of Noah. Noah was a righteous man, blameless in his time; Noah walked with God. ¹⁰Noah became the father of three sons: Shem, Ham, and Japheth.
>
> ¹¹Now the earth was corrupt in the sight of God, and the earth was filled with violence. ¹²God looked on the earth, and behold, it was corrupt; for all flesh had corrupted their way upon the earth.
>
> ¹³Then God said to Noah, "The end of all flesh has come before Me; for the earth is filled with violence because of them; and behold, I am about to destroy them with the earth. ¹⁴"Make for yourself an ark of gopher wood; you shall make the ark with rooms, and shall cover it inside and out with pitch. ¹⁵"This is how you shall make it: the length of the ark three hundred cubits, its breadth fifty cubits, and its height thirty cubits. ¹⁶"You shall make a window for the ark, and finish it to a cubit from the top; and set the door of the ark in the side of it; you shall make it with lower, second, and third decks. ¹⁷"Behold, I, even I am bringing the flood of water upon the earth, to destroy all flesh in which is the breath of life, from under heaven; everything that is on the earth shall perish. ¹⁸"But I will establish My covenant with you; and you shall enter the ark—you and your sons and your wife, and your sons' wives with you. ¹⁹"And of every living thing of all flesh, you shall bring two of every *kind* into the ark, to keep *them* alive with you; they shall be male and female. ²⁰"Of the birds after their kind, and of the animals after their kind, of every creeping thing of the ground after its kind, two of every *kind* will come to you to keep *them* alive. ²¹"As for you, take for yourself some of all food which is edible, and gather *it* to yourself; and it shall be for food for you and for them." ²²Thus Noah did; according to all that God had commanded him, so he did. (Genesis 6:5-22)

Noah and a Trusting Faith

2. You will read more of the story in the next two layers, but let's dig a little in the part of Noah's story you read today. Look back in verse 5 and see why God was going to flood the earth. Write what you see below.

It is hard to think about how bad things must have been, isn't it? God said that the thoughts of men's hearts were evil. Then He added the word "continually." That means that man was thinking evil thoughts all of the time! Sounds like the world was a sad place, doesn't it?

3. Look in verse 6 and see how God felt about how men were acting. Write two things you find about God's feelings.

4. But now let's see how God felt about Noah. Note from verse 8 what Noah found with God.

Do you know what it means to find favor with a person? It means that God was pleased with Noah. Noah was the favorite! But there was a good reason he was. You will see!

5. Dig just a little deeper, and then we will take a break. Look in verse 9 and find three facts about Noah. Note each below.

-
-
-

6. Did you notice that one of these facts is the same thing you discovered about Enoch? Which of the facts about Noah is the same as one of the truths you unearthed about Enoch?

Good. Both of these men walked with God! You can see, can't you, why Noah was favored? He walked with God! Think about that treasure and take a fun break. You have worked so hard to reach the bottom of this layer that I bet you are ready for some outdoor fun! And I think you certainly deserve that!

See you in Layer Two. I am excited to continue the story with you as we dig further into Noah's faith!

LAYER TWO: Walking All Alone

Are you excited to dig deeper into the story of Noah? I am! Even though I know the story I am excited to read it again and see what new treasure I uncover. So, let's get digging!

1. Continue digging into the story of Noah by carefully reading the verses below.

1Then the LORD said to Noah, "Enter the ark, you and all your household, for you *alone* I have seen *to be* righteous before Me in this time. **2**"You shall take with you of every clean animal by sevens, a male and his female; and of the animals that are not clean two, a male and his female; **3**also of the birds of the sky, by sevens, male and female, to keep offspring alive on the face of all the earth. **4**"For after seven more days, I will send rain on the earth forty days and forty nights; and I will blot out from the face of the land every living thing that I have made." **5**Noah did according to all that the LORD had commanded him.

6Now Noah was six hundred years old when the flood of water came upon the earth. **7**Then Noah and his sons and his wife and his sons' wives with him entered the ark because of the water of the flood....

Noah and a Trusting Faith

¹²The rain fell upon the earth for forty days and forty nights.

¹³On the very same day Noah and Shem and Ham and Japheth, the sons of Noah, and Noah's wife and the three wives of his sons with them, entered the ark,…

¹⁸The water prevailed and increased greatly upon the earth, and the ark floated on the surface of the water. ¹⁹The water prevailed more and more upon the earth, so that all the high mountains everywhere under the heavens were covered. ²⁰The water prevailed fifteen cubits higher, and the mountains were covered. ²¹All flesh that moved on the earth perished, birds and cattle and beasts and every swarming thing that swarms upon the earth, and all mankind; ²²of all that was on the dry land, all in whose nostrils was the breath of the spirit of life, died. ²³Thus He blotted out every living thing that was upon the face of the land, from man to animals to creeping things and to birds of the sky, and they were blotted out from the earth; and only Noah was left, together with those that were with him in the ark. ²⁴The water prevailed upon the earth one hundred and fifty days. (Genesis 7:1-7, 12-13, 18-24)

2. Notice in verse 1 that God tells Noah it is time to go into the ark. Then, look in verses 12-13 and see what happened on the day God told them to get in the ark. Write what you see.

God told Noah at the perfect moment that it was time to get in the ark. Don't you think that's neat? We are going to talk later about Noah's faith, so don't forget this little treasure you just discovered.

3. Isn't it really sad that man didn't trust God or follow Him? Read what God did in verse 23. Remember as you read that you have already discovered that man was evil. Write below what you see about what happened to man.

4. Go back and look in verse 23 to see what is said about Noah. Write it below.

5. Can you imagine you and your family being the only people left on the entire earth? Hard to think about what that would be like, isn't it? But think about why Noah was left. Write what you think.

Yes, Noah walked with God. Even when everyone else around him was evil and doing what they wanted to do, Noah did what God wanted him to do. It is hard to think about what it would be like to walk with God when no one else is—when walking with God means you are the ONLY one going that way. I think that would take a special kind of faith, don't you?

Remember, too, that Noah, in faith, had to build a boat for a flood when no one had ever seen rain! I am sure people thought he was really nuts at that point. Then he had to take his family and two of every animal and close himself up in the boat! If people did not think he was nuts before, I am certain that now they thought he had gone totally crazy!

Think about what you have dug out today. Look at the pile of dirt you have left from all of your hard work and grab the truths you have unearthed. The truth that Noah walked with God when no one else did is an amazing one! You should be excited about discovering it!

Today, in this moment, ask God to help you be a guy or gal who will walk with Him even when others don't! Remember, it will take faith to do that, but God will build your faith if that is what you really want.

LAYER THREE: A Bow to Remember

In this layer, you will get to the bottom of the story about Noah. I think we should dig through to the bottom now, just so you can be reminded how the story ends. Then, in the next layer, we are going to zero in on the truths you've found and see what we can learn about his faith from the story you have worked through in the first three layers.

1. Read the rest of the story, then we will work our way back through the entire story.

[13]Now it came about in the six hundred and first year, in the first *month,* on the first of the month, the water was dried up from the earth. Then Noah removed the covering of the ark, and looked, and behold, the surface of the ground was dried up. [14]In the second month, on the twenty-seventh day of the month, the earth was dry. [15]Then God spoke to Noah, saying, [16]"Go out of the ark, you and your wife and your sons and your sons' wives with you. [17]"Bring out with you every living thing of all flesh that is with you, birds and animals and every creeping thing that creeps on the earth, that they may breed abundantly on the earth, and be fruitful and multiply on the earth." [18]So Noah went out, and his sons and his wife and his sons' wives with him. (Genesis 8:13-18)

[8]Then God spoke to Noah and to his sons with him, saying, [9]"Now behold, I Myself do establish My covenant with you, and with your descendants after you; [10]and with every living creature that is with you, the birds, the cattle, and every beast of the

Noah and a Trusting Faith

earth with you; of all that comes out of the ark, even every beast of the earth. **11**"I establish My covenant with you; and all flesh shall never again be cut off by the water of the flood, neither shall there again be a flood to destroy the earth." **12**God said, "This is the sign of the covenant which I am making between Me and you and every living creature that is with you, for all successive generations; **13**I set My bow in the cloud, and it shall be for a sign of a covenant between Me and the earth. **14**"It shall come about, when I bring a cloud over the earth, that the bow will be seen in the cloud, **15**and I will remember My covenant, which is between Me and you and every living creature of all flesh; and never again shall the water become a flood to destroy all flesh. **16**"When the bow is in the cloud, then I will look upon it, to remember the everlasting covenant between God and every living creature of all flesh that is on the earth." (Genesis 9:8-16)

2. So, when the water was gone, God had Noah and all who were in the ark come out. God then made a covenant to Noah. A covenant is a promise. Look in verse 11 and write below what God promised.

3. Read verses 13-15 again, and write out what sign God said would be a reminder of the promise.

Now, every time you see a rainbow, you can think about this story and God's faithfulness to keep His promise—and you can think of Noah's faith to do what God told him to do. In fact, that is what we are going to examine more carefully in the next layer! See you there!

LAYER FOUR: A Big Boat and No Water!

As we begin to dig today, I want to think back on the treasure you have uncovered in the first three layers. We are going to examine some of it more carefully and pick out some other treasures that we haven't gotten to yet. Ready? Good.

1. Think about the fact that the story of Noah is recorded in chapter 6 of Genesis—almost the very beginning of the Word of God. When I thought about that, I went back and read Genesis 1–5 to see what had happened from the beginning to this point in time. Relax, I am not going to ask you to do that!

But, as I read, I had an interesting thought I wanted to share with you. I think it will help in understanding the kind of faith Noah had. Think about this: In all of the record of man, up to the point of Noah and the flood, it had not rained on the earth!

I know your question may be: "How did the plants get water if it had not rained." Well, if you will look at the verse below, I think you will find your answer.

But a mist used to rise from the earth and water the whole surface of the ground.
(Genesis 2:6)

God is amazing, isn't He? He had a way for the plants to be watered that did not involve rain. So, I think from this verse and from the fact that there is no mention of rain in Genesis 1–5, we can assume it had not rained. Man did not know what rain was!

2. Now think about Noah and the fact that God told him to build an ark because it was going to flood. How do you think Noah felt? It is hard to imagine! But what did Noah do?

3. Yes, he built the ark. Why?

Right again, because he walked with God and had the kind of faith that trusted God no matter what. He had faith that what God said was true and right. Noah could not begin to understand what a flood would be like, but in his trusting faith he obeyed.

Noah and a Trusting Faith

And, don't forget, Noah also had to be willing to lock his family and lots of animals in the ark when God said to—even though it was not even raining yet!

4. Let's dig into two verses where you will uncover a neat truth about Noah and his faith. Read the verses below and note what you learn about Noah.

Thus Noah did; according to all that God had commanded him, so he did. (Genesis 6:22)

Noah did according to all that the LORD had commanded him. (Genesis 7:5)

Yes, he did *all* that God told him to do. Noah trusted God and obeyed all He said! He did not try to figure out if God was right. He did not try to think about what may work better than an ark—like treading water.

Wouldn't you like to have a faith that trusts what God says even if it does not make sense to your logic or what you know? We will talk more about Noah's faith in Layer Five. See you there!

LAYER FIVE: Noah's Reverence is Rewarded

Are you thinking carefully about the faith Noah had in his God? I think looking at what God records about him in the faith hall of fame will help.

1. Read Hebrews 11:7 and think about what you have discovered so far as you read.

By faith Noah, being warned *by God* about things not yet seen, in reverence prepared an ark for the salvation of his household, by which he condemned the world, and became an heir of the righteousness which is according to faith. (Hebrews 11:7)

2. You see that Noah was warned about things "not yet seen." What did God warn him of that had never been seen?

Right, the flood! No rain to this point!

3. Go back and read Hebrews 11:7 and note carefully the first two words of the verse. Why did Noah build the ark?

Yes, because he had faith in God. He trusted what God said.

4. There are two other words that I think we need to look at in this verse. These words are "in reverence." Do you know what reverence means? Look it up in a dictionary and write the meaning below.

Yes, reverence is respect. Noah had a respect for God. Again, you see he trusted God—even when he couldn't imagine what a flood would be like since it had never rained!

5. Because Noah trusted and obeyed, his household was saved. From what we saw in the story, we know that God was going to destroy man and the world as it was, so why does the verse say Noah condemned the world? Think about it and write your idea.

I think Noah condemned the world because he walked with God and was a man of trusting faith. If no one had lived like Noah, then all men would have been alike—evil. But Noah's faith showed that man could believe God and walk with Him! And, don't forget, Noah was the only man walking with God! He was all alone in his faith!
Don't you want to become a man or woman who walks with God and trusts and obeys Him? Ask Him to show you how to become that man or woman!
We have talked about some things you can do right now to begin walking with God and building your faith, so I know you are on your way if that is what you want. Why don't you

take some time today and talk with your parents about becoming a person of trusting faith? I know they would really like to talk with you about that!

6. As you enjoy the fact that you completed this amazing dig, turn to page 68 and work the great puzzle there!

7. Don't forget to record three "Truth Treasures."

I am so proud of you! I would take you out for a treat if I was there with you! But I hope you will take time now to do something that you enjoy. Since the leaves are falling outside as I am talking to you, I am going for a walk in the crisp air. Do something fun outside in the season and get ready for Dig Six soon!

Truth Treasures for the Week

1.

2.

3.

Bury the Treasure:

Trust in the Lord with all of your heart, and do not lean on your own understanding. In all your ways acknowledge Him, and He will make your paths straight. (Proverbs 3:5)

Truth Trackers: Heroes of Faith

Noah Crossword Puzzle

You've learned a lot about Noah in this dig. See how much you can remember! Find a place for each word in the squares below. If you get stuck, look back through the chapter for help.

Across

3. Rain fell on the earth for _____ days and nights
5. Birds and _____ were also on the ark
6. Noah found _____ in God's eyes
7. Noah's grandfather
8. Noah was a _____ man
9. An ark is a _____
10. A kind of promise
12. Noah _____ with God

Down

1. Noah fathered three sons: Shem, Ham, and _____
2. Before the flood, _____ had never fallen from the sky
4. Another word for respect
6. Noah had a trusting _____
9. God's reminder of His promise
11. Noah built an _____

solution on page 165

Dig 6

Abraham and His Believing Faith

Tools of the Trade

1. Colored pencils
2. Pen or pencil
3. Game on page 82

Directions for Diggers

I'm glad you are back to go digging! I am super ready to head off on this dig. When you find out whose faith we are digging into this time, you will be excited, too! It is Abraham! I have heard him called the "father of our faith," and after this dig you will see why.

I have a friend who lives in Israel, and his job is to welcome people who travel to "the land of the Bible" and show them around. His name is Abraham, and he is a tour guide. Often, the groups he leads will sing a song to him that they learned when they were younger because he makes them think of father Abraham. Do you know the song? It goes like this:

"Father Abraham had many sons, many sons had father Abraham. I am one of them and so are you, so let's just praise the Lord."

You sing this over and over louder and louder and faster and faster. It is fun! But every time I hear this little song I think of father Abraham's amazing faith. I bet after you dig through his story and learn about his faith that you will, too.

Okay, let's hit it!

LAYER ONE: Moving Day Is Coming!

The story recorded about Abraham is long—like the one about Noah—so it will take some time to dig through it. But we will talk about his faith as we dig, and I know you will be excited to see how he believed God—no matter what.

1. Read Genesis 12:1-5 and think carefully about what God is truly saying to Abraham. God asks some incredible things of him, but he also makes an awesome promise at the same time.

¹Now the LORD said to Abram,
"Go forth from your country,
And from your relatives
And from your father's house,
To the land which I will show you;
²And I will make you a great nation,
And I will bless you,
And make your name great;
And so you shall be a blessing;
³And I will bless those who bless you,
And the one who curses you I will curse.
And in you all the families of the earth will be blessed."
⁴So Abram went forth as the LORD had spoken to him; and Lot went with him. Now Abram was seventy-five years old when he departed from Haran. ⁵Abram took Sarai his wife and Lot his nephew, and all their possessions which they had accumulated, and the persons which they had acquired in Haran, and they set out for the land of Canaan; thus they came to the land of Canaan. (Genesis 12:1-5)

2. God tells Abraham he is going to be moving! What does God tell him to leave? Look at verse 1 and list the three things he is to leave.

-
-
-

Abraham and His Believing Faith

So, God tells Abraham it is time to move, but Abraham has to give up his home country, his family, and his parents! You will see that some of his relatives go with him, but he must have had to leave many behind because of what God says here.

3. Just after God tells Abraham what he must leave behind, God then tells him what He is going to do with him if he obeys. List below what God is planning for Abraham. You will see these promises in verses 2-3, and you will have a long list when you note all of them. So, take your time and think—and be sure you list everything.

-
-
-
-
-
-
-

Can you even begin to realize what God has said to this man who becomes the "father of our faith"? God has told Abraham that he is going to become a great nation. Out of that nation, something will happen that will be a blessing to all the families of the earth. I don't know about you, but my head would be spinning if I had been Abraham. And I would have had tons of questions!

But we don't hear questions from Abraham! Abraham left and did what God said. He trusted God enough to pack up and leave his family, his parents, and his home and head off to parts unknown with only a promise! He didn't have a written contract that promised a return trip if things didn't work out! Now *that* is faith—a faith that believed God even when it could not see the land or imagine what could possibly happen that would make a great nation from one man!

Think about this kind of faith and decide if you would like to have it. Remember, Abraham had to believe and, in faith, had to act! He had to do all that God asked in order for God to do what He promised!

Truth Trackers: Heroes of Faith

LAYER TWO: Stars and Sand, or People?

We are already on Layer Two! Let's get started right away since there is so much to dig through. We are going to continue to dig and think about Abraham's faith!

1. Remember that we left Abraham yesterday with lots of promises from God. But there were some things Abraham had to do, too. And he had to have the faith to believe God would do what He promised if he did what God asked him to do.

In this layer, you are going to see that Abraham left his home and eventually came to the land God had promised to him. Let's see what God said to him when he arrived.

14The LORD said to Abram, after Lot had separated from him, "Now lift up your eyes and look from the place where you are, northward and southward and eastward and westward; **15**for all the land which you see, I will give it to you and to your descendants forever. **16**"I will make your descendants as the dust of the earth, so that if anyone can number the dust of the earth, then your descendants can also be numbered. **17**"Arise, walk about the land through its length and breadth; for I will give it to you." **18**Then Abram moved his tent and came and dwelt by the oaks of Mamre, which are in Hebron, and there he built an altar to the LORD.
(Genesis 13:14-18)

2. First you see that Abraham's nephew, who had traveled with him, was going now to live in a separate place. Then you read how God talked to Abraham about the land and gave it to Abraham just as He had promised.

What does God say to Abraham about his descendants—about the children and grandchildren and great-grandchildren he will have? Look in verse 16 and write what God says about them.

3. What does God mean? He explains what He is saying. Read verse 16 again and write below how many descendants Abraham would have.

Again, God talks to Abraham about all the people who will come from him. In this verse God tells Abraham there will be so many that no one can number them. God had kept His promise about the land, and now He is talking about another promise.

4. Read Genesis 17:5-8 below.

⁵"No longer shall your name be called Abram,
But your name shall be Abraham;
For I will make you the father of a multitude of nations.
⁶"I will make you exceedingly fruitful, and I will make nations of you, and kings will come forth from you. ⁷"I will establish My covenant between Me and you and your descendants after you throughout their generations for an everlasting covenant, to be God to you and to your descendants after you. ⁸"I will give to you and to your descendants after you, the land of your sojournings, all the land of Canaan, for an everlasting possession; and I will be their God." (Genesis 17:5-8)

Yes, Abraham will be the father of many nations! God had already told Abraham that He would do something special through one nation, but now He is telling him that there will be many! And God promises that He will keep the land He is giving to Abraham and give it to his descendants!

5. In verse 7, what does God promise to be to Abraham—and to all those who will be his children and grandchildren and great-grandchildren and on and on?

Right! He promises to be their God! Now you can see why Abraham is called the "father of our faith"—father Abraham. God said that Abraham would be the man He used to start nations full of many people who would believe in God! And Abraham's believing faith would be the beginning of all that!

6. Hey, why don't you try your hand at the neat puzzle on page 82, and then call it good for the day!

Don't forget all the things you are learning in this dig, but let's take a break. I don't want to exhaust you! I know you may want to dig deeper, but we'll hit Layer Three hard as soon as you are back! See you in Layer Three!

LAYER THREE: One Son = Many Nations!

Oh, I am glad you are back! I am eager to get deeper into Abraham's story, so let's dig!

1. Did you catch the fact in the last layer that Abraham was seventy-five years old when God asked him to leave his home and go to an unknown country? Abraham lived for one hundred more years, but he was not a young man when God began to stretch his faith!

Read from Genesis 17 and see what God says to Abraham twenty-four years later. As you read, look for what God promises Abraham now when he is ninety-nine years old.

15Then God said to Abraham, "As for Sarai your wife, you shall not call her name Sarai, but Sarah *shall be* her name. **16**"I will bless her, and indeed I will give you a son by her. Then I will bless her, and she shall be *a mother of* nations; kings of peoples will come from her." **17**Then Abraham fell on his face and laughed, and said in his heart, "Will a child be born to a man one hundred years old? And will Sarah, who is ninety years old, bear *a child?*" (Genesis 17:15-17)

2. What does God say is going to happen?

WOW! That is a lot to believe, isn't it? Remember, Abraham is ninety-nine years old now! Abraham really had to have a faith that believed! Abraham trusted God and continued to act—no matter how impossible it seemed to have a son!

Remember, Abraham already had seen God give him the land He had promised!

Abraham must have been blown away! Believing what God said meant Abraham had to believe something that seemed impossible! What did he have to believe that seemed impossible? Read verses 15-17 again and write below what you find.

Yes, Abraham had to believe that even though he would be one hundred years old God could give him a son! People were older in Abraham's time when they had children than we are now, but one hundred years old was too old to have a child. And that is just what Abraham thought!

3. What does he do in response to God's promise? Read verse 17. Does he say anything to God?

No, he just says it in his heart, doesn't he? I don't think Abraham laughed because he didn't believe God. I think he was just shocked that this was the thing that was going to happen next!

4. Why is the promise of a son important? Why did Abraham need a son? Think hard and write out your thoughts below.

You are right again! If God was going to make Abraham the father of many nations, he had to have lots of children! He needed a son so that this big family could get started. And there was going to be a son—the son that God promised! The son would have Abraham as a father and Abraham's wife, Sarah, as his mom!

Stop now and think of the kind of faith Abraham had to have! He had to believe in a country he had never seen and leave all that he knew to go there. Then he had to believe that God could give an old man a son! God is asking a lot, isn't He? But Abraham knows God, and he decides to believe Him again. He had a faith that believed and a faith that acted on what it believed!

In Layer Four we will keep digging to see what else we can learn about this believing faith! Meet you there soon!

LAYER FOUR: A Miracle Baby!

Have you recovered from the last dig? I think that is the deepest layer we have had to work through yet in this dig. But you were awesome, and you made it!

I hope you are ready because you are about to find some amazing treasures! Let's dig so you can see what God did with Abraham.

1. Read Genesis 21:2-3,5 and write below what God did.

²So Sarah conceived and bore a son to Abraham in his old age, at the appointed time of which God had spoken to him. ³Abraham called the name of his son who was born to him, whom Sarah bore to him, Isaac…. ⁵Now Abraham was one hundred years old when his son Isaac was born to him. (Genesis 21:2-3,5)

2. Did God come through on His second promise to Abraham?

3. What did Abraham name his son?

4. Now you are about to dig out an awesome truth, so hang in there and let's dig! Read the verses below from Genesis 22 and think carefully as you read. I know it is long, but you will be amazed at what happens now!

1Now it came about after these things, that God tested Abraham, and said to him, "Abraham!" And he said, "Here I am." **2**He said, "Take now your son, your only son, whom you love, Isaac, and go to the land of Moriah, and offer him there as a burnt offering on one of the mountains of which I will tell you." **3**So Abraham rose early in the morning and saddled his donkey, and took two of his young men with him and Isaac his son; and he split wood for the burnt offering, and arose and went to the place of which God had told him…. **6**Abraham took the wood of the burnt offering and laid it on Isaac his son, and he took in his hand the fire and the knife. So the two of them walked on together. **7**Isaac spoke to Abraham his father and said, "My father!" And he said, "Here I am, my son." And he said, "Behold, the fire and the wood, but where is the lamb for the burnt offering?" **8**Abraham said, "God will provide for Himself the lamb for the burnt offering, my son." So the two of them walked on together. **9**Then they came to the place of which God had told him; and Abraham built the altar there and arranged the wood, and bound his son Isaac and laid him on the altar, on top of the wood. **10**Abraham stretched out his hand and took the knife to slay his son. **11**But the angel of the LORD called to him from heaven and said, "Abraham, Abraham!" And he said, "Here I am." **12**He said, "Do not stretch out your hand against the lad, and do nothing to him; for now I know that you fear God, since you have not withheld your son, your only son, from Me." **13**Then Abraham raised his eyes and looked, and behold, behind *him* a ram caught in the thicket by his horns; and Abraham went and took the ram and offered him up for a burnt offering in the place of his son. (Genesis 22:1-3, 6-13)

5. What does God ask Abraham to do with Isaac? Look in verse 2 and write below what you see.

6. Why does God ask Abraham to do this? The key to this question is in verse 1.

Abraham and His Believing Faith

Yes, God tested Abraham. You and I are convinced by now that Abraham had a believing faith, but God wanted to see Abraham's faith in action again. And this was a hard thing to ask, wasn't it?

It was hard to ask not just because Isaac was Abraham and Sarah's only son and they loved him very much. It was hard because God had said that Abraham would be the father of many nations, of a multitude of descendants, and he needed a son for all of that to happen!

7. When Isaac asks Abraham what is going to happen, what does his father say to him? Write Abraham's response from verse 8 below.

8. Abraham believed God, didn't he? I am sure he could not figure out all that was happening either, but he knew God had made a promise and given Isaac to him. So Abraham continued to believe and act in faith!

Read verses 9-10 again to see how far Abraham was willing to go. What was he about to do?

9. What happens that stops Abraham? Write what you see in verses 11-12.

10. What does Abraham see that he offers to God? Read verse 13 again.

Abraham had amazing faith, didn't he? He knew what God had promised, and he knew it could not happen without a son! In Layer Five we will learn something else about Abraham's faith when God asks him to offer Isaac. But today, think about Abraham's faith and think about yours. Do you have the kind of faith that believes God and acts on what He says? If you want this kind of faith, ask God to grow it in your heart!

Take time this afternoon to talk with your mom or dad about this layer and all that you dug out! I know they would be excited to talk with you about Abraham's faith! Maybe you can make a treat and invite them to share it with you while you talk. Peanut butter and crackers sounds good to me, so I am off.

Catch you in Layer Five!

LAYER FIVE: A Dead Man Becomes a Dad?

Today we will dig through several more verses and discover some truths that will help put together the pieces of the puzzle about Abraham's faith. Guess where these verses are? Hebrews 11—the faith hall of fame! I know you're not surprised that Abraham is listed there in light of all you have unearthed in the first four layers!

1. Read Hebrews 11:8-12, 17-19 on the next page.

⁸By faith Abraham, when he was called, obeyed by going out to a place which he was to receive for an inheritance; and he went out, not knowing where he was going. ⁹By faith he lived as an alien in the land of promise, as in a foreign *land*, dwelling in tents with Isaac and Jacob, fellow heirs of the same promise; ¹⁰for he was looking for the city which has foundations, whose architect and builder is God. ¹¹By faith even Sarah herself received ability to conceive, even beyond the proper time of life, since she considered Him faithful who had promised. ¹²Therefore there was born even of one man, and him as good as dead at that, *as many descendants* as the stars of heaven in number, and innumerable as the sand which is by the seashore....

¹⁷By faith Abraham, when he was tested, offered up Isaac, and he who had received the promises was offering up his only begotten *son;* ¹⁸*it was he* to whom it was said, "In Isaac your descendants shall be called." ¹⁹He considered that God is able to raise *people* even from the dead, from which he also received him back as a type. (Hebrews 11:8-12, 17-19)

The story told in these verses probably sounds familiar to you since you have spent four layers digging out Abraham's story in Genesis. But let's examine more closely a couple of truths you have already discovered, and let's dig out new treasures!

2. You already know that Abraham was one hundred when Isaac was born, but dig in verse 12 and see what it says about Abraham's age. Read carefully and write below what it says about how old he was.

Abraham and His Believing Faith

I think it's interesting that it says Abraham "was as good as dead"! Now that is old to have a son! Just think again about what God did. He gave a son to a man who was one hundred! But also think about the faith it took to believe God when He said what He was going to do!

3. Dig in verse 12 and see how many children it says were born to this man, Abraham. It does not just talk about Isaac being born, it talks about all of the descendants to come. How many were there?

Have you ever walked on the beach? Think about how much sand you could see and feel with your toes! Or have you ever camped in an area where the sky was open and you could see a zillion stars overhead?

This verse says that the people who were born through Abraham are more than all of the sand on the beach and more than all of the stars in the sky. Now that is a lot!

4. Let's dig out one last truth—a new one. Look in verse 19 and see what it says Abraham considered.

Yes, he decided that God could raise Isaac from the dead if necessary. Abraham believed several things:

- Abraham believed God would do what He said about nations and descendants.

- Abraham believed God had given him Isaac, who would have his descendants.

- Abraham believed God had told him to offer Isaac.

- Abraham believed that if he obeyed God and offered Isaac that God would raise Isaac from the dead to keep His promise!

Amazing faith, isn't it—faith that believed there was a land and left home, faith that believed there would be a nation, faith that believed the son was to give birth to the nation, faith that believed God would not fail to do what He said!

5. Have you wondered how the nation was used to bless all the earth—another of the promises you listed in Layer One? Well, think with me. What person is the biggest blessing to mankind in all of history? Right, Jesus! He came to die for our sins and blessed us with eternal life. He is the descendant of Abraham who would bless the world!

Guess which nation Jesus was born in? Yes, Israel—the nation that Abraham's descendants lived in when Jesus was born, and the nation they live in today!

6. Record your "Truth Treasures."

Abraham believed, in faith, and God did all that He said He would do for Abraham! You can have this believing faith, too. You don't need a lot of faith to do big things— you just need a believing faith!

TRUTH TREASURES FOR THE WEEK

1.

2.

3.

BURY THE TREASURE:

If you had faith like a mustard seed, you would say to this mulberry tree, "Be uprooted and be planted in the sea;" and it would obey you. (Luke 17:6)

Abraham and His Believing Faith

A Constellation Promise

God promised that Abraham would have "as many descendants as the stars." Hidden in this maze is another promise that God made to Abraham. To discover this promise, find the path through these stars, filling in the blanks as you go. (This will help you to make sure you're on the right path!) Hint: Avoid the letters B, J, P, Q, V, X, and Z.

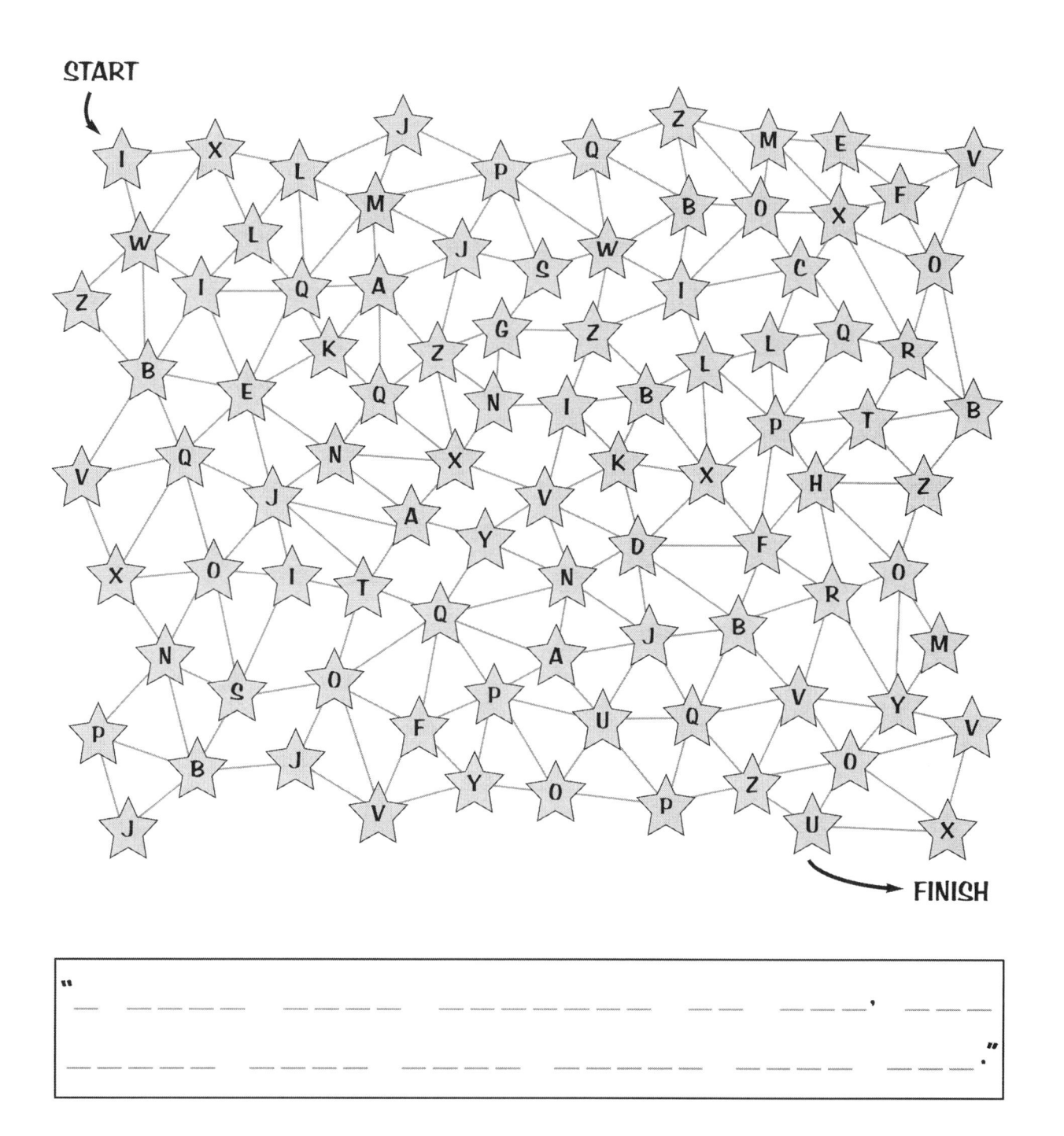

solution on page 165

Dig 7

Sarah's Confident Faith

Tools of the Trade

1. Colored pencils
2. Pen or pencil
3. Game on page 90

Directions for Diggers

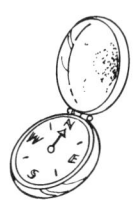

This will be the first dig where we will examine the faith of a woman. Her name is Sarah. Do you remember whose wife she is? Now, this is harder, but can you remember her son's name?

Well, if you remembered that Sarah was Abraham's wife you have a good memory. And if you remembered that the son she and Abraham had was Isaac, you have an amazing memory!

I hope you are excited to look at the faith of this wonderful woman whose faith was worthy of being noted in Hebrews 11.

Pack up and let's head out!

LAYER ONE: Sarah Laughs

Sarah's story is a fun one to read. You will recognize some of it since she is Abraham's wife. You read some of her story when you dug into his life, but let's read about Sarah and see what you can discover about her—and about her faith!

Truth Trackers: Heroes of Faith

1. Read Genesis 18:1-15 and focus on what you see about Sarah. As you read, use your yellow pencil and circle her name and what you see about her.

1Now the LORD appeared to him by the oaks of Mamre, while he was sitting at the tent door in the heat of the day. **2**When he lifted up his eyes and looked, behold, three men were standing opposite him; and when he saw them, he ran from the tent door to meet them and bowed himself to the earth, **3**and said, "My lord, if now I have found favor in your sight, please do not pass your servant by. **4**"Please let a little water be brought and wash your feet, and rest yourselves under the tree; **5**and I will bring a piece of bread, that you may refresh yourselves; after that you may go on, since you have visited your servant." And they said, "So do, as you have said." **6**So Abraham hurried into the tent to Sarah, and said, "Quickly, prepare three measures of fine flour, knead it and make bread cakes." **7**Abraham also ran to the herd, and took a tender and choice calf and gave it to the servant, and he hurried to prepare it. **8**He took curds and milk and the calf which he had prepared, and placed it before them; and he was standing by them under the tree as they ate.

9Then they said to him, "Where is Sarah your wife?" And he said, "There, in the tent." **10**He said, "I will surely return to you at this time next year; and behold, Sarah your wife will have a son." And Sarah was listening at the tent door, which was behind him. **11**Now Abraham and Sarah were old, advanced in age; Sarah was past childbearing. **12**Sarah laughed to herself, saying, "After I have become old, shall I have pleasure, my lord being old also?" **13**And the LORD said to Abraham, "Why did Sarah laugh, saying, 'Shall I indeed bear a child, when I am so old?' **14**"Is anything too difficult for the LORD? At the appointed time I will return to you, at this time next year, and Sarah will have a son." **15**Sarah denied it however, saying, "I did not laugh"; for she was afraid. And He said, "No, but you did laugh." (Genesis 18:1-15)

2. What do the men who came to visit Abraham and Sarah say is going to happen in a year? Look in verse 10 and write what you find below.

3. Look in verse 12 and note what Sarah did when she heard what was said.

4. Do you remember what Abraham did once when God told him he was going to have a son when he was one hundred years old?

Yes, he laughed too, didn't he? I am sure it was really hard to believe! Now Sarah does the same—she laughs!

5. Look back in verse 12 and see why Sarah laughed.

Yes, she knew she was too old—and she knew Abraham was too old also!

6. When the visitors hear Sarah laugh, they make an amazing statement! Look in verse 14 and write below what they said.

Don't you think that is a great statement? Nothing is too hard for God! Don't ever forget that statement and when it was made!

When she was asked why she laughed, Sarah said that she had not laughed! She was afraid that the visitors would wonder if she believed God! But the men did not let her get away with that statement. They said again, "Yes, you laughed." I am sure this made Sarah think about her faith and if she truly believed. It would make me think about mine. Don't you think you would, too? But I think she laughed for the same reason Abraham laughed: It was thrilling to think a son was on the way, and, yes, it was hard to believe after all these years!

Speaking of your faith, ask God to give you more faith as you dig into the faith of all of these men and women of Hebrews 11! He will!

Good job. See you in Layer Two!

LAYER TWO: A Miracle Comes to Life!

1. Begin today by reading what happens to Sarah a year later.

¹Then the LORD took note of Sarah as He had said, and the LORD did for Sarah as He had promised. **²**So Sarah conceived and bore a son to Abraham in his old age, at the appointed time of which God had spoken to him. **³**Abraham called the name of his son who was born to him, whom Sarah bore to him, Isaac. (Genesis 21:1-3)

2. What happens?

3. When does it happen? Look carefully.

Yes, "the appointed time," which means it happened exactly when the men had said—a year later.

God did exactly what He said He would do. And He did it exactly when He said He would do it. God does not fail! He is a God who deserves our faith. In the next layer we will talk more about Sarah's laughter and about her faith. See you there soon!

LAYER THREE: The Joy of a Baby

1. Now read what Sarah says about this event.

⁶Sarah said, "God has made laughter for me; everyone who hears will laugh with me." ⁷And she said, "Who would have said to Abraham that Sarah would nurse children? Yet I have borne him a son in his old age." (Genesis 21:6-7)

2. Sarah talks about laughter again. Now it is clearly a laughter of joy! What does she say everyone will do?

Yes, she knows other people will be happy for her and for Abraham. She says they will laugh, too!

3. Read Genesis 17:19 and see what God had told Abraham earlier about the baby's name. What did God say to name him?

But God said, "No, but Sarah your wife will bear you a son, and you shall call his name Isaac; and I will establish My covenant with him for an everlasting covenant for his descendants after him." (Genesis 17:19)

4. If you spoke Hebrew and could read the Old Testament in the language in which it was first written, you would realize that the name Abraham and Sarah gave this miracle baby means laughter. Yes, Isaac means laughter!

Why do you think God told Abraham and Sarah to name him "laughter"? Write your idea.

Sarah's Confident Faith

I think his name was Isaac because God gave them this son who He had promised was such a joy that he brought laughter to them! God was filled with joy that they had believed Him, and they were filled with joy that their faith had been rewarded! God told them He was going to do something that was impossible. They believed Him—and He did it. And the fact that their faith was in a faithful God brought them great joy!

Think about the fact that God was faithful. That means He always did what He said He would do. Do you believe God will do what He says? In Layer Four we are going to talk more about God's faithfulness.

See you in Layer Four soon.

LAYER FOUR: God Is Faithful!

1. Read Hebrews 11:11 to see what is said about Sarah in the faith hall of fame!

By faith even Sarah herself received ability to conceive, even beyond the proper time of life, since she considered Him faithful who had promised. (Hebrews 11:11)

2. Do you know what it means when it says she "received the ability to conceive"? Write what you think it means.

If you said that it means she received the ability to have a baby, you are right! Remember, Sarah was too old to have a baby, but God said she would. This verse says that by faith she received the ability to have a baby! Sarah had Isaac because she believed God. She had confidence that He could do what He said He would do. And not only did she believe He *could* do it, she believed that He *would* do it!

3. What did you dig out of this verse about Sarah's faith? What do you find about what Sarah considered?

That is correct. She considered God faithful to do what He promised!

4. Take a minute and look at the puzzle on page 90. Looks like fun, doesn't it? Go for it!

Ask God to give you a faith that believes He is faithful!

Truth Trackers: Heroes of Faith

LAYER FIVE: A Confident Faith

You may have lots of ideas about God and what He will and won't do, but you need to learn all you can about who He really is and how He really works so you can have a strong *faith* in Him. I think that digging out truths about these men and women of faith will help build your faith! So, you are on your way to building a strong and powerful faith!

Now you have come to the last layer of another great dig! I am proud of you for your diligence and your willingness to work hard to dig out truth treasures.

1. Let's start by talking more about Sarah's faith. I think I can help you see what kind of faith she had by using an illustration that you will understand because it happens to you every day!

In the morning when you come to breakfast, do you sit in a chair at the table? Or, when you get to school, do you have a desk you sit in every day? Well, when you get ready to sit down, do you stop and think every time about whether the chair or desk will hold you? Do you wonder every time you sit down if you are going to crash to the floor?

Or do you just sit down because you believe that you are going to be held up? That is my guess. You have confidence in the fact that the chair or desk will hold you. You do not need to stop and decide if you can sit without ending up on the floor every time you sit.

That is the kind of faith Sarah had. She was confident because she had faith in a faithful God. She knew He would act and do what He said, even though what He had said was impossible in human terms. She did not worry. She just sat down with confidence!

Don't you want to have a confident faith that believes God will always act as He says—that believes He is faithful? Ask God to work in your heart to help you see who He is, so you can be confident in His faithfulness and have a confident faith like Sarah!

2. Write out a short prayer to God and tell Him about the kind of faith you want to have. You can also think back about the faith you have uncovered in the other digs: Abel's obedient faith, Enoch's devoted faith, Noah trusting faith, Abraham's obedient faith, and now, Sarah's confident faith!

3. And now don't forget your "Truth Treasures."

Well, you have reached the bottom, and I am so proud of you! Go out and have some fun and take a nice break before Dig Eight!

Truth Treasures for the Week

1.

2.

3.

Bury the Treasure:

Know therefore that the Lord your God, He is God, the faithful God, who keeps His covenant…to a thousand generations with those who love Him and keep His commandments.

(Deuteronomy 7:9)

An Alphanumber Promise

There are numbers in each square of the diagram below. The numbers represent letters of the alphabet. Change the numbers to letters and discover one of promises Jesus gave to Abraham and Sarah.

A 1	B 2	C 3	D 4	E 5	F 6	G 7	H 8	I 9	J 10	K 11	L 12	M 13	N 14
O 15	P 16	Q 17	R 18	S 19	T 20	U 21	V 22	W 23	X 24	Y 25	Z 26	Space 27

9	19	27	1	14	25	20	8	9	14	7
27	20	15	15	27	4	9	6	6	9	3
21	12	20	27	6	15	18	27	20	8	5
27	12	15	18	4	?	...	1	20	27	20
8	9	19	27	20	9	13	5	27	14	5
24	20	27	25	5	1	18	...	19	1	18
1	8	27	23	9	12	12	27	8	1	22
5	27	1	27	19	15	14	27			Genesis 18:14

"__ _____ ___ _____ ___ ___ _____? ...

__ ____ ____ ... _____ ____ _____ __ ____."

solution on page 166

Dig 8

Joseph's Steadfast Faith

Tools of the Trade

1. Colored pencils
2. Pen or pencil
3. Dictionary
4. Game on page 106

Directions for Diggers

Today you are going to meet a man whose faith was tested in many ways. When we first meet this man, he is just a young boy. His dad has given him a special gift—a coat of many colors.

This young boy becomes a mighty man of faith. He is a great example of one who could have become angry with God because things didn't go his way. Instead, he believed that God was faithful, and he waited to see what God would do to bring him out of the bad situation he was in. His faith did not change just because he found himself in some tough places. Joseph was a man of steadfast faith who continued to believe God no matter what!

Check in with headquarters, and let's meet Joseph. I will tell you that you'll do lots of hard, long digging in this dig, but it will be so worth it!

Truth Trackers: Heroes of Faith

LAYER ONE: The Dreamer

First, let me tell you about a special find, and then we will jump into the story of Joseph!

Special Find: You're going to read a lot in this dig about a guy called Pharoah. You may know all about the Pharaohs because you may have studied about them in school. But in case you haven't, "Pharoah" is a title for a man who held the office of the top ruler in Egypt—sort of like the president of the United States.

1. You may already know about Joseph, but, even if you do, I am excited about sharing his story with you again. I know you will uncover some new finds as you go! Read Genesis 37:1-11 to see what is happening with Joseph when his dad gives him the multi-colored coat.

> ¹Now Jacob lived in the land where his father had sojourned, in the land of Canaan. ²These are *the records of* the generations of Jacob.
> Joseph, when seventeen years of age, was pasturing the flock with his brothers while he was *still* a youth, along with the sons of Bilhah and the sons of Zilpah, his father's wives. And Joseph brought back a bad report about them to their father. ³Now Israel loved Joseph more than all his sons, because he was the son of his old age; and he made him a varicolored tunic. ⁴His brothers saw that their father loved him more than all his brothers; and *so* they hated him and could not speak to him on friendly terms.
> ⁵Then Joseph had a dream, and when he told it to his brothers, they hated him even more. ⁶He said to them, "Please listen to this dream which I have had; ⁷for behold, we were binding sheaves in the field, and lo, my sheaf rose up and also stood erect; and behold, your sheaves gathered around and bowed down to my sheaf." ⁸Then his brothers said to him, "Are you actually going to reign over us? Or are you really going to rule over us?" So they hated him even more for his dreams and for his words.
> ⁹Now he had still another dream, and related it to his brothers, and said, "Lo, I have had still another dream; and behold, the sun and the moon and eleven stars were bowing down to me." ¹⁰He related *it* to his father and to his brothers; and his father rebuked him and said to him, "What is this dream that you have had? Shall I and your mother and your brothers actually come to bow ourselves down before you to the ground?" ¹¹His brothers were jealous of him, but his father kept the saying *in mind.* (Genesis 37:1-11)

2. Why did Joseph's brothers dislike him? Look in verse 4.

Joseph's Steadfast Faith

3. What happens in verse 5 that makes matters even worse?

4. What does verse 11 say about how Joseph's brothers felt about him?

So, Joseph was just a young guy when he was favored by his father and when he had a dream that he believed meant he would rule over his brothers someday.

5. Let's keep digging and see what else we can find about Joseph at this time in his life. Read Genesis 37:12-28.

¹²Then his brothers went to pasture their father's flock in Shechem. ¹³Israel said to Joseph, "Are not your brothers pasturing *the flock* in Shechem? Come, and I will send you to them." And he said to him, "I will go." ¹⁴Then he said to him, "Go now and see about the welfare of your brothers and the welfare of the flock, and bring word back to me." So he sent him from the valley of Hebron, and he came to Shechem.

¹⁵A man found him, and behold, he was wandering in the field; and the man asked him, "What are you looking for?" ¹⁶He said, "I am looking for my brothers; please tell me where they are pasturing *the flock.*" ¹⁷Then the man said, "They have moved from here; for I heard *them* say, 'Let us go to Dothan.'" So Joseph went after his brothers and found them at Dothan.

¹⁸When they saw him from a distance and before he came close to them, they plotted against him to put him to death. ¹⁹They said to one another, "Here comes this dreamer! ²⁰"Now then, come and let us kill him and throw him into one of the pits; and we will say, 'A wild beast devoured him.' Then let us see what will become of his dreams!" ²¹But Reuben heard *this* and rescued him out of their hands and said, "Let us not take his life." ²²Reuben further said to them, "Shed no blood. Throw him into this pit that is in the wilderness, but do not lay hands on him"—that he might rescue him out of their hands, to restore him to his father. ²³So it came about, when Joseph reached his brothers, that they stripped Joseph of his tunic, the varicolored tunic that was on him; ²⁴and they took him and threw him into the pit. Now the pit was empty, without any water in it.

²⁵Then they sat down to eat a meal. And as they raised their eyes and looked, behold, a caravan of Ishmaelites was coming from Gilead, with their camels bearing aromatic gum and balm and myrrh, on their way to bring *them* down to Egypt. ²⁶Judah said to his brothers, "What profit is it for us to kill our brother and cover up his blood? ²⁷"Come and let us sell him to the Ishmaelites and not lay our hands on him, for he is our brother, our *own* flesh." And his brothers listened *to him.* ²⁸Then

some Midianite traders passed by, so they pulled *him* up and lifted Joseph out of the pit, and sold him to the Ishmaelites for twenty *shekels* of silver. Thus they brought Joseph into Egypt. (Genesis 37:12-28)

6. Joseph's dad had him check to see how his brothers were doing. What did they do when they saw him coming? Look at verse 18.

7. What do they call Joseph in verse 19?

8. Read verses 21-22 again to see what Reuben, one of the brothers, suggested. Write it below.

9. What did the brothers do in verses 23-24?

10. Another brother, Judah, suggested a plan, and the brothers followed it. What did they do in verses 26-27?

11. Let's read a little more of the story and dig for a few more treasures. Then you will be able to take a break. Read Genesis 37:29-36.

²⁹Now Reuben returned to the pit, and behold, Joseph was not in the pit; so he tore his garments. ³⁰He returned to his brothers and said, "The boy is not *there*; as for me, where am I to go?" ³¹So they took Joseph's tunic, and slaughtered a male goat and dipped the tunic in the blood; ³²and they sent the varicolored tunic and brought it to their father and said, "We found this; please examine *it* to *see* whether it is your son's tunic or not." ³³Then he examined it and said, "It is my son's tunic. A wild beast has devoured him; Joseph has surely been torn to pieces!" ³⁴So Jacob tore his clothes,

and put sackcloth on his loins and mourned for his son many days. ³⁵Then all his sons and all his daughters arose to comfort him, but he refused to be comforted. And he said, "Surely I will go down to Sheol in mourning for my son." So his father wept for him. ³⁶Meanwhile, the Midianites sold him in Egypt to Potiphar, Pharaoh's officer, the captain of the bodyguard. (Genesis 37:29-36)

12. How did the brothers try to hide what they had done?

13. Did their father believe that Joseph was dead?

14. What does verse 36 say happened to Joseph?

I am sure Joseph thought his dream was from God and that God had shown him he would one day rule over his brothers! But then his brothers turned on him and even sold him to traders who took him to Egypt. That sure would shake my confidence that the dream was from God. Wouldn't you wonder how you would rule over your brothers from a foreign country? Let's take a break and then come back soon in Layer Two to see if Joseph is shaken by these events.

LAYER TWO: The Prisoner

Let's start digging right away to see what Joseph does now that he is in such a mess!

1. Read Genesis 39:1-6.

¹Now Joseph had been taken down to Egypt; and Potiphar, an Egyptian officer of Pharaoh, the captain of the bodyguard, bought him from the Ishmaelites, who had taken him down there. ²The LORD was with Joseph, so he became a successful man. And he was in the house of his master, the Egyptian. ³Now his master saw that the LORD was with him and *how* the LORD caused all that he did to prosper in his hand. ⁴So Joseph found favor in his sight and became his personal servant; and he made him overseer over his house, and all that he owned he put in his charge. ⁵It came about that from the time he made him overseer in his house and over all that he

owned, the LORD blessed the Egyptian's house on account of Joseph; thus the LORD's blessing was upon all that he owned, in the house and in the field. **6**So he left everything he owned in Joseph's charge; and with him *there* he did not concern himself with anything except the food which he ate.

Now Joseph was handsome in form and appearance. (Genesis 39:1-6)

2. When Joseph arrived in Egypt, how did things go for him?

3. Go back and read the verses in number 1 again. This time, use your red colored pencil and draw a cross over the word "Lord" every time you see it used in these verses.

4. Now, look at what is said each time the word "Lord" is used. Who do you think was in charge of all that was happening?

5. Next, let's read Genesis 39:7-20. Hang in there. See how strong Joseph was!

7It came about after these events that his master's wife looked with desire at Joseph, and she said, "Lie with me." **8**But he refused and said to his master's wife, "Behold, with me *here,* my master does not concern himself with anything in the house, and he has put all that he owns in my charge. **9**"There is no one greater in this house than I, and he has withheld nothing from me except you, because you are his wife. How then could I do this great evil and sin against God?" **10**As she spoke to Joseph day after day, he did not listen to her to lie beside her *or* be with her. **11**Now it happened one day that he went into the house to do his work, and none of the men of the household was there inside. **12**She caught him by his garment, saying, "Lie with me!" And he left his garment in her hand and fled, and went outside. **13**When she saw that he had left his garment in her hand and had fled outside, **14**she called to the men of her household and said to them, "See, he has brought in a Hebrew to us to make sport of us; he came in to me to lie with me, and I screamed. **15**"When he heard that I raised my voice and screamed, he left his garment beside me and fled and went outside." **16**So she left his garment beside her until his master came home. **17**Then she spoke to him with these words, "The Hebrew slave, whom you brought to us, came in to me to make sport of me; **18**and as I raised my voice and screamed, he left his garment beside me and fled outside."

19Now when his master heard the words of his wife, which she spoke to him, saying, "This is what your slave did to me," his anger burned. **20**So Joseph's master took him and put him into the jail, the place where the king's prisoners were confined; and he was there in the jail. (Genesis 39:7-20)

6. Did Joseph do anything wrong?

7. Did he do anything right?

8. Where did Joseph end up?

9. Was that fair?

10. Does all this mean that God was no longer in control?

11. Do you think Joseph had a reason to believe that God was not in control?

12. Did Joseph let go of his faith in God?

13. Now take a look at Genesis 39:21-23.

²¹But the Lord was with Joseph and extended kindness to him, and gave him favor in the sight of the chief jailer. ²²The chief jailer committed to Joseph's charge all the prisoners who were in the jail; so that whatever was done there, he was responsible *for it*. ²³The chief jailer did not supervise anything under Joseph's charge because the Lord was with him; and whatever he did, the Lord made to prosper. (Genesis 39:21-23)

14. Again mark the word "Lord" like you did before. Who was in charge?

15. What happened to Joseph?

16. Read more of the story now in Genesis 40:1-14.

¹Then it came about after these things, the cupbearer and the baker for the king of Egypt offended their lord, the king of Egypt. **²**Pharaoh was furious with his two officials, the chief cupbearer and the chief baker. **³**So he put them in confinement in the house of the captain of the bodyguard, in the jail, the *same* place where Joseph was imprisoned. **⁴**The captain of the bodyguard put Joseph in charge of them, and he took care of them; and they were in confinement for some time. **⁵**Then the cupbearer and the baker for the king of Egypt, who were confined in jail, both had a dream the same night, each man with his *own* dream *and* each dream with its *own* interpretation. **⁶**When Joseph came to them in the morning and observed them, behold, they were dejected. **⁷**He asked Pharaoh's officials who were with him in confinement in his master's house, "Why are your faces so sad today?" **⁸**Then they said to him, "We have had a dream and there is no one to interpret it." Then Joseph said to them, "Do not interpretations belong to God? Tell *it* to me, please."

⁹So the chief cupbearer told his dream to Joseph, and said to him, "In my dream, behold, *there was* a vine in front of me; **¹⁰**and on the vine *were* three branches. And as it was budding, its blossoms came out, *and* its clusters produced ripe grapes. **¹¹**"Now Pharaoh's cup was in my hand; so I took the grapes and squeezed them into Pharaoh's cup, and I put the cup into Pharaoh's hand." **¹²**Then Joseph said to him, "This is the interpretation of it: the three branches are three days; **¹³**within three more days Pharaoh will lift up your head and restore you to your office; and you will put Pharaoh's cup into his hand according to your former custom when you were his cupbearer. **¹⁴**"Only keep me in mind when it goes well with you, and please do me a kindness by mentioning me to Pharaoh and get me out of this house. (Genesis 40:1-14)

17. What did Joseph do for the cupbearer? (If you want to know about the baker, you can get your Bible and read the rest of the story in Genesis 40.)

18. What did Joseph ask the cupbearer to do?

19. Skip to the end of Genesis 40 and read verse 23 to see what the cupbearer did. Write what you find below.

The chief jailer did not supervise anything under Joseph's charge because the LORD was with him; and whatever he did, the LORD made to prosper. (Genesis 39:23)

If God is in control, isn't it hard to imagine why things keep going so wrong for Joseph? Keep your eye on him, though, and think about how he responds. Think about his faith, that he did not turn back or blame God!

LAYER THREE: The Administrator

Yes, there is more Scripture to read today, but aren't you interested in this story? I think it is one of the very best in the Bible! I am excited when I think about how God wants to work in your life and help you become a person of steadfast faith.

1. By the way, do you know what the word "steadfast" means? Okay, look it up in your dictionary and write the definition below. This word will help you as you continue to dig out things about Joseph's faith and examine them.

So, you can see that it means his faith did not go up and down and back and forth because of all that was happening. His faith stayed steady—steadfast!

2. Let's look in Genesis 41:1-14.

¹Now it happened at the end of two full years that Pharaoh had a dream, and behold, he was standing by the Nile. ²And lo, from the Nile there came up seven cows, sleek and fat; and they grazed in the marsh grass. ³Then behold, seven other cows came up after them from the Nile, ugly and gaunt, and they stood by the *other* cows on the bank of the Nile. ⁴The ugly and gaunt cows ate up the seven sleek and fat cows. Then Pharaoh awoke. ⁵He fell asleep and dreamed a second time; and behold, seven ears of grain came up on a single stalk, plump and good. ⁶Then behold, seven ears, thin and scorched by the east wind, sprouted up after them. ⁷The thin ears swallowed up the seven plump and full ears. Then Pharaoh awoke, and behold, *it was* a dream. ⁸Now in the morning his spirit was troubled, so he sent and called for all the magicians of Egypt, and all its wise men. And Pharaoh told them his dreams, but there was no one who could interpret them to Pharaoh.

⁹Then the chief cupbearer spoke to Pharaoh, saying, "I would make mention today of my *own* offenses. ¹⁰"Pharaoh was furious with his servants, and he put me in confinement in the house of the captain of the bodyguard, *both* me and the chief baker. ¹¹"We had a dream on the same night, he and I; each of us dreamed according to the interpretation of his *own* dream. ¹²"Now a Hebrew youth *was* with us there, a servant of the captain of the bodyguard, and we related *them* to him, and he interpreted our dreams for us. To each one he interpreted according to his *own* dream. ¹³"And just as he interpreted for us, so it happened; he restored me in my office, but he hanged him."

14Then Pharaoh sent and called for Joseph, and they hurriedly brought him out of the dungeon; and when he had shaved himself and changed his clothes, he came to Pharaoh. (Genesis 41:1-14)

3. How many years have passed?

4. What happened to make the cupbearer remember Joseph?

5. Now Joseph is brought to Pharaoh and told about his dreams. Just as before, God helped Joseph explain what the dreams meant—that there were to be seven years of plenty and seven years of famine. Let's read more.

39So Pharaoh said to Joseph, "Since God has informed you of all this, there is no one so discerning and wise as you are. **40**"You shall be over my house, and according to your command all my people shall do homage; only in the throne I will be greater than you." **41**Pharaoh said to Joseph, "See, I have set you over all the land of Egypt." **42**Then Pharaoh took off his signet ring from his hand and put it on Joseph's hand, and clothed him in garments of fine linen and put the gold necklace around his neck. **43**He had him ride in his second chariot; and they proclaimed before him, "Bow the knee!" And he set him over all the land of Egypt. **44**Moreover, Pharaoh said to Joseph, "*Though* I am Pharaoh, yet without your permission no one shall raise his hand or foot in all the land of Egypt." **45**Then Pharaoh named Joseph Zaphenath-paneah; and he gave him Asenath, the daughter of Potiphera priest of On, as his wife. And Joseph went forth over the land of Egypt. **46**Now Joseph was thirty years old when he stood before Pharaoh, king of Egypt. And Joseph went out from the presence of Pharaoh and went through all the land of Egypt. **47**During the seven years of plenty the land brought forth abundantly. **48**So he gathered all the food of *these* seven years which occurred in the land of Egypt and placed the food in the cities; he placed in every city the food from its own surrounding fields. **49**Thus Joseph stored up grain in great abundance like the sand of the sea, until he stopped measuring *it,* for it was beyond measure. **50**Now before the year of famine came, two sons were born to Joseph, whom Asenath, the daughter of Potiphera priest of On, bore to him. (Genesis 41:39-50)

6. What did Pharaoh do for Joseph?

7. What did Joseph do once he was in this new position? Why did he do it?

8. Now read the end of Genesis 41.

⁵³When the seven years of plenty which had been in the land of Egypt came to an end, ⁵⁴and the seven years of famine began to come, just as Joseph had said, then there was famine in all the lands, but in all the land of Egypt there was bread. ⁵⁵So when all the land of Egypt was famished, the people cried out to Pharaoh for bread; and Pharaoh said to all the Egyptians, "Go to Joseph; whatever he says to you, you shall do." ⁵⁶When the famine was *spread* over all the face of the earth, then Joseph opened all the storehouses, and sold to the Egyptians; and the famine was severe in the land of Egypt. ⁵⁷*The people of* all the earth came to Egypt to buy grain from Joseph, because the famine was severe in all the earth. (Genesis 41:53-57)

9. Did God do what He said in Pharaoh's dreams that He would do?

10. How widespread was the famine?

Are you beginning to see that God is in control even when it may not look like He is? Remember when we looked at the faith of others noted in Hebrews 11 that we have talked about God's faithfulness? Again, in Joseph's story, you see that God is faithful— He has a plan for Joseph, and He is working it out even though we can't see how. And because Joseph believed God, he knew this was true. He surely couldn't see what was going to happen!

LAYER FOUR: The Brother

1. Now, let's look at the rest of the story! Read Genesis 42:1-3.

¹Now Jacob saw that there was grain in Egypt, and Jacob said to his sons, "Why are you staring at one another?" ²He said, "Behold, I have heard that there is grain in Egypt; go down there and buy *some* for us from that place, so that we may live and not die." ³Then ten brothers of Joseph went down to buy grain from Egypt. (Genesis 42:1-3)

2. When the brothers came to Egypt to buy grain, it was necessary for them to appear before Joseph. When they bowed before him, he recognized them and remembered the dreams he had as a young boy. But his brothers did not recognize him as a grown man—especially since he was a ruler in a foreign land!

Joseph had them thrown in jail as spies. He later heard them expressing their sorrow for having sold him into slavery. Then he came up with a plan. He ordered that one of the brothers be held in prison and that the other nine go home and bring back the youngest brother, Benjamin, who had stayed at home with Jacob, their father.

Jacob had been tremendously grieved by the loss of Joseph, and now he thought he had lost another son to a prison in Egypt! He refused to allow the youngest to return to Egypt with his brothers. He did not want to lose him, too!

But the famine got worse, so Jacob was forced to allow Benjamin to return to Egypt with the others. They needed food! Joseph was greatly touched by the sight of his brother, Benjamin. He brought the brothers into his own house and fed them.

Then Joseph had another plan. He ordered his servant to fill their sacks with grain and to place his silver cup in Benjamin's sack. Finally, the brothers left for home. On their way back, the brothers were stopped by Joseph's men. These men accused them of stealing. When the sacks were searched, they found the cup in Benjamin's sack.

One of the brothers, Judah, was very upset. He had promised his father he would bring Benjamin home unharmed. So he pleaded with Joseph for mercy. He told him how sad their father would be if he lost another son.

3. Read Genesis 45:1-11

1Then Joseph could not control himself before all those who stood by him, and he cried, "Have everyone go out from me." So there was no man with him when Joseph made himself known to his brothers. **2**He wept so loudly that the Egyptians heard *it*, and the household of Pharaoh heard *of it*. **3**Then Joseph said to his brothers, "I am Joseph! Is my father still alive?" But his brothers could not answer him, for they were dismayed at his presence.

4Then Joseph said to his brothers, "Please come closer to me." And they came closer. And he said, "I am your brother Joseph, whom you sold into Egypt. **5**"Now do not be grieved or angry with yourselves, because you sold me here, for God sent me before you to preserve life. **6**"For the famine *has been* in the land these two years, and there are still five years in which there will be neither plowing nor harvesting. **7**"God sent me before you to preserve for you a remnant in the earth, and to keep you alive by a great deliverance. ⁸"Now, therefore, it was not you who sent me here, but God; and He has made me a father to Pharaoh and lord of all his household and ruler over all the land of Egypt. ⁹"Hurry and go up to my father, and say to him, 'Thus says your son Joseph, "God has made me lord of all Egypt; come down to me, do not delay. ¹⁰"You shall live in the land of Goshen, and you shall be near me, you and your children and your children's children and your flocks and your herds and all that you have. ¹¹"There I will also provide for you, for there are still five years of famine *to come,* and you and your household and all that you have would be impoverished."' (Genesis 45:1-11)

4. Did Joseph hold a grudge against his brothers for what they had done to him?

5. Who did Joseph say sent him to Egypt?

6. How did God cause all the circumstances to work for good for Joseph?

7. How did God cause everything to work for good for his family?

8. Who was in control of what happened to Joseph?

If Joseph had not been in Egypt, his family would not have had food! God knew all that was happening and He knew the end of the story!

9. There is a puzzle on page 106 that will be great fun for you! Go for it!

If you will remember that God is in control—even when things may look out of control—your faith will not be shaky. If you will learn who God is and how He works, your faith will become strong and steadfast!

LAYER FIVE: The Provider

Let's look now at the short reference to Joseph in Hebrews 11. It is only one verse, but what it says is BIG!

1. Read Hebrews 11:22.

By faith Joseph, when he was dying, made mention of the exodus of the sons of Israel, and gave orders concerning his bones. (Hebrews 11:22)

2. This verse says something very important about Joseph. It tells us that his faith was steadfast all the way to the end of his life! You may wonder what I mean and how I arrive at that conclusion, so let me tell you. You will have to think hard with me for a moment.

Remember Abraham and the promise God made to him about a land and a people? Well, the people God was talking about with Abraham are Joseph and his family! Yes, his brothers and their father and all their children are those people. They ended up in Egypt when the famine hit, and that is where they found their brother, Joseph.

While they lived in Egypt, the family grew and grew. And Joseph knew that there was a land that they would go back to one day. As he dies, he has the faith to mention the exodus of the children of Israel—his family. He knows God will take them out of Egypt one day and back to the land that was promised to Abraham! He has steadfast faith to believe that what God promised will happen—even though he will not see it!

3. What does it say Joseph requested concerning his bones?

Yes, he wanted his grave to be moved when the children of Israel left Egypt. He wanted to go home, too!

4. Don't forget your "Truth Treasures"!

Aren't you just amazed that Joseph never went back and forth in his faith, even though his world turned upside down? Ask God to grow a steadfast faith in your heart so that, no matter what happens, you will remember that God is in control. He is working so that everything will work for good for you! He is an amazing God, and He is worthy of a steadfast faith! He is faithful!

Truth Treasures for the Week

1.

2.

3.

Bury the Treasure:

And we know that God causes all things to work together for good to those who love God, to those who are called according to His purpose. (Romans 8:28)

Truth Trackers: Heroes of Faith

Name Game

Unscramble the names of the nine key people in the story of this dig. Pay close attention, because two of them are particularly tricky! They were mentioned in the story, but not by name. Once you've unscrambled the words, use the numbers to uncover a truth about Joseph.

Scrambled Name   **Unscrambled Name**

1. B O A J C   __ __ __ __ __
                12   8

2. A H A R H O P   __ __ __ __ __ __ __
                    11   14

3. R A B E K   __ __ __ __ __
               22

4. O H S J E P   __ __ __ __ __ __
                 16

5. A P I O T P H R   __ __ __ __ __ __ __
               2   4

6. J E B N A N I M   __ __ __ __ __ __ __ __
              1   26 24

7. E B A R C U R P E   __ __ __ __ __ __ __ __
            21   20

8. U B E N E R   __ __ __ __ __ __
          3

9. H U D J A   __ __ __ __ __
           17 9

"__ __ __   L __ __ __   W __   W __ __   __ __ __;
 4 11 22   14 3 9   20 16   24 4 11   11 24 26

__ __ __   W __ __ __ __   V __   __ __   __ __ __,   __ __ __
20 1 9   11 20 4 22   22 3   11 22   9 24 9   4 11 22

L __ __   __ __ __ __ __ __ __ __ __ __ __."
14 3 9   26 20 9 22   4 14   2 3 14 16 2 22 3

(Genesis 39:23)

solution on page 166

106

Dig 9

Moses' Fearless Faith

Tools of the Trade

1. Colored pencils
2. Pen or pencil
3. Game on page 120

Directions for Diggers

Today we begin to dig through Scripture about one of my favorite Bible characters! There are lots of reasons that I like the story about Moses, but I don't want to tell you why yet. I want you to see what you think, then at the end of our dig I will tell you why I like the story.

I bet you probably know a lot about Moses. Because there is so much about him in the Bible, we won't read it all. But we will hit the highlights and see what we can dig out about his faith. This dig will require lots of digging—just like Dig Eight—but, again, it is really worth it!

Don't forget to check in with headquarters, and then we're outta here!

LAYER ONE: Hidden Baby

Okay, now that we are on our site, let's begin our exciting dig about Moses. I think you know the story about Moses when he was a baby, but let's dig through it and see what new treasure you uncover.

1. Read Exodus 1:22–2:10. Take your time and think as you dig through these verses so you can answer the questions that follow.

> **22**Then Pharaoh commanded all his people, saying, "Every son who is born you are to cast into the Nile, and every daughter you are to keep alive."
> **1**Now a man from the house of Levi went and married a daughter of Levi. **2**The woman conceived and bore a son; and when she saw that he was beautiful, she hid him for three months. **3**But when she could hide him no longer, she got him a wicker basket and covered it over with tar and pitch. Then she put the child into it and set *it* among the reeds by the bank of the Nile. **4**His sister stood at a distance to find out what would happen to him.
> **5**Then the daughter of Pharaoh came down to bathe at the Nile, with her maidens walking alongside the Nile; and she saw the basket among the reeds and sent her maid, and she brought it *to her*. **6**When she opened *it,* she saw the child, and behold, *the* boy was crying. And she had pity on him and said, "This is one of the Hebrews' children." **7**Then his sister said to Pharaoh's daughter, "Shall I go and call a nurse for you from the Hebrew women that she may nurse the child for you?" **8**Pharaoh's daughter said to her, "Go *ahead.*" So the girl went and called the child's mother. **9**Then Pharaoh's daughter said to her, "Take this child away and nurse him for me and I will give *you* your wages." So the woman took the child and nursed him. **10**The child grew, and she brought him to Pharaoh's daughter and he became her son. And she named him Moses, and said, "Because I drew him out of the water." (Exodus 1:22–2:10)

2. What was Pharaoh's order about the babies being born?

Pharaoh was having babies killed because he said the Israelites were becoming too strong. He thought he could make them weak if they did not have baby boys to grow up into strong men and have more children.

3. When Moses was born, his mother hid him in her home for three months. But when she couldn't hide him any longer, what did she do?

4. Who took the basket to the Nile River?

5. Who found that basket in the river?

6. When Pharaoh's daughter found the baby, what did Moses' sister say to her?

7. Whom did the sister get to take care of the baby?

So you see that Moses' mother was able to have more time with him and to care for him until he was older.

This is how Moses began his life. Can you see that his mother was a woman of faith herself? She believed that she could care for her son and hide him as an infant. When he was three months old, she had the faith to put him in a basket in the Nile, believing someone would find him and care for him. Then, her faith was rewarded by Moses' being returned to her, and she was allowed to take care of him until he was older!

Moses had a legacy of faith—just like Noah had a legacy of faith! Do you remember that Noah's grandfather was also a man of faith? If you are a guy or gal of faith, one day when you have a family they will want to be strong in faith because of what they see in your life. How exciting!

We will talk more about faith as we dig! Think today, though, about a woman whose faith saved her son's life!

See you in Layer Two.

LAYER TWO: Defender of His People

We are going to dig more in this layer to see what the Bible says about Moses, and we will see what you can discover about his faith. Let's start digging where we stopped yesterday!

1. Read Exodus 2:11-16 and work through the questions that follow.

11Now it came about in those days, when Moses had grown up, that he went out to his brethren and looked on their hard labors; and he saw an Egyptian beating a Hebrew, one of his brethren. **12**So he looked this way and that, and when he saw there was no one *around,* he struck down the Egyptian and hid him in the sand. **13**He went out the next day, and behold, two Hebrews were fighting with each other; and he said to the offender, "Why are you striking your companion?" **14**But he said, "Who made you a prince or a judge over us? Are you intending to kill me as you killed the Egyptian?" Then Moses was afraid and said, "Surely the matter has become known."

15When Pharaoh heard of this matter, he tried to kill Moses. But Moses fled from the presence of Pharaoh and settled in the land of Midian, and he sat down by a well.

16Now the priest of Midian had seven daughters; and they came to draw water and filled the troughs to water their father's flock. (Exodus 2:11-16)

2. When Moses was grown up, what did he see happening one day?

3. What did he do about it?

You may wonder exactly what it means when the Bible says, "he struck down the Egyptian." But if you look at the next part of the verse that says Moses "hid him in the sand," you probably realize that Moses killed the man and buried him!

4. What happens that makes Moses realize other people know about the man he killed?

5. What does Pharaoh do?

6. What does Moses do then? Where does he go to live?

Moses' Fearless Faith

7. Let's dig a little deeper and see what happens when Moses settles in Midian. Read Exodus 2:16-22 and write below what Moses does.

> **16**Now the priest of Midian had seven daughters; and they came to draw water and filled the troughs to water their father's flock. **17**Then the shepherds came and drove them away, but Moses stood up and helped them and watered their flock. **18**When they came to Reuel their father, he said, "Why have you come *back* so soon today?" **19**So they said, "An Egyptian delivered us from the hand of the shepherds, and what is more, he even drew the water for us and watered the flock." **20**He said to his daughters, "Where is he then? Why is it that you have left the man behind? Invite him to have something to eat." **21**Moses was willing to dwell with the man, and he gave his daughter Zipporah to Moses. **22**Then she gave birth to a son, and he named him Gershom, for he said, "I have been a sojourner in a foreign land." (Exodus 2:16-22)

8. Now that Moses is married and has a son, something interesting happens in Egypt. Read the verses below carefully and see what happens to the Pharaoh (he is called the king). Also look to see what God does.

> **23**Now it came about in *the course of* those many days that the king of Egypt died. And the sons of Israel sighed because of the bondage, and they cried out; and their cry for help because of *their* bondage rose up to God. **24**So God heard their groaning; and God remembered His covenant with Abraham, Isaac, and Jacob. **25**God saw the sons of Israel, and God took notice *of them.* (Exodus 2:23-25)

9. What happened to Pharaoh?

10. What does verse 24 say that God remembers?

Do you remember that God had made a promise to Abraham about a nation and a land? Well, the people who are to become the nation are in bondage in Egypt, and the land He promised is far away!

11. What does verse 25 say that God does?

Truth Trackers: Heroes of Faith

Okay, I know you can't really see yet how Moses' faith plays into this picture. But meet me soon in Layer Three and you will!

LAYER THREE: Called by God

1. Read Exodus 3:1-12.

¹Now Moses was pasturing the flock of Jethro his father-in-law, the priest of Midian; and he led the flock to the west side of the wilderness and came to Horeb, the mountain of God. ²The angel of the Lord appeared to him in a blazing fire from the midst of a bush; and he looked, and behold, the bush was burning with fire, yet the bush was not consumed. ³So Moses said, "I must turn aside now and see this marvelous sight, why the bush is not burned up." ⁴When the Lord saw that he turned aside to look, God called to him from the midst of the bush and said, "Moses, Moses!" And he said, "Here I am." ⁵Then He said, "Do not come near here; remove your sandals from your feet, for the place on which you are standing is holy ground." ⁶He said also, "I am the God of your father, the God of Abraham, the God of Isaac, and the God of Jacob." Then Moses hid his face, for he was afraid to look at God.

⁷The Lord said, "I have surely seen the affliction of My people who are in Egypt, and have given heed to their cry because of their taskmasters, for I am aware of their sufferings. ⁸"So I have come down to deliver them from the power of the Egyptians, and to bring them up from that land to a good and spacious land, to a land flowing with milk and honey, to the place of the Canaanite and the Hittite and the Amorite and the Perizzite and the Hivite and the Jebusite. ⁹"Now, behold, the cry of the sons of Israel has come to Me; furthermore, I have seen the oppression with which the Egyptians are oppressing them.

¹⁰"Therefore, come now, and I will send you to Pharaoh, so that you may bring My people, the sons of Israel, out of Egypt." ¹¹But Moses said to God, "Who am I, that I should go to Pharaoh, and that I should bring the sons of Israel out of Egypt?" ¹²And He said, "Certainly I will be with you, and this shall be the sign to you that it is I who have sent you: when you have brought the people out of Egypt, you shall worship God at this mountain." (Exodus 3:1-12)

Moses is a shepherd and is taking care of the flock when God appears to him. He was just doing his normal job!

2. How does God appear?

Moses' Fearless Faith

3. What does Moses do in verse 6 when he realizes he is talking with God?

4. In verse 8, why does God say He has come down?

5. What does God tell Moses He wants him to do in helping to save His people? Look in verse 10.

Don't forget that we are talking about the people and land that God promised Abraham. God is faithful! And now He is going to build the faith of a man named Moses so that he becomes a part of God's plan for this people and the land He wants them to live in!

6. Getting exciting, isn't it? Read Exodus 3:19-20 to see what God tells Moses about how difficult the task will be.

¹⁹"But I know that the king of Egypt will not permit you to go, except under compulsion. ²⁰"So I will stretch out My hand and strike Egypt with all My miracles which I shall do in the midst of it; and after that he will let you go. (Exodus 3:19-20)

7. What does God say the new king of Egypt is going to do?

8. What does God say He will do? Look in verse 20.

9. Does He say anything about what the king will do after that?

10. Now, let's dig and see what God does with Moses to build his faith.

¹Then Moses said, "What if they will not believe me or listen to what I say? For they may say, 'The Lord has not appeared to you.'" ²The Lord said to him, "What is that in your hand?" And he said, "A staff." ³Then He said, "Throw it on the ground." So

he threw it on the ground, and it became a serpent; and Moses fled from it. **4**But the LORD said to Moses, "Stretch out your hand and grasp *it* by its tail"—so he stretched out his hand and caught it, and it became a staff in his hand— **5**"that they may believe that the LORD, the God of their fathers, the God of Abraham, the God of Isaac, and the God of Jacob, has appeared to you." (Exodus 4:1-5)

11. God tells Moses to throw his staff (or cane) on the ground. What happens when Moses throws it down?

12. What does God tell Moses now?

13. And what happens?

Now that would build my faith! Would it build yours? At the end of this talk with God, Moses sees that there is nothing to fear if he does what God says to do!

You're doing great! See you tomorrow!

LAYER FOUR: Challenger of Pharaoh

If I didn't think it would exhaust you, we'd dig in each Scripture that talks about Moses coming to Pharaoh and telling him to let the people go. You would discover that every time Moses came, Pharaoh would not let the people go. Moses had to go back again and again and face this cruel king.

1. The first time Pharaoh did not cooperate, the water of the Nile River turned to blood. Do you live near a river or have you ever seen one? Can you imagine seeing it flow with blood? That would scare me into letting the Israelites go, but not Pharoah!

2. The second time Moses went before Pharaoh, again Pharaoh wouldn't let the people go, so the land was covered with frogs! Frogs in the bathtub! Frogs in the bed! Frogs in everyone's cereal bowls! Frogs everywhere!

3. Next, there were lice all over. Lice are little insects that infect people's hair and spread disease.

4. Then flies covered everyone and every inch of the land! Have you ever had a fly pester you at a picnic? Can you imagine being covered with these buzzing creatures? That's what Pharaoh and the Egyptians experienced.

5. Next the livestock died. This was their livelihood—their horses, donkeys, camels, cattle, sheep, and goats.

6. Then a horrible thing happened in which the people and the animals were covered with awful sores called boils. But still after all this, Pharaoh *still* wouldn't let the people go!

7. When all these failed, God rained down hail. Have you ever been in a hail storm? It can be scary!

8. Then large, ugly, loud insects called locusts covered the land! Creepy! The Bible says that there were so many locusts that the ground could not even be seen. Pharaoh was still not moved. He was not willing to let the people go!

9. God then made the land dark for three days. Just the other night, in the town where I was spending the night, the lights went out. They stayed out for over an hour! It was kind of eerie not to be able to see anything! And for three days and nights it was dark in the land of Egypt!

10. Finally, the last and most terrible plague came: All of the firstborn children and animals died! The Israelites had been told by God what to do so that the angel of death would pass over their homes—so that none of their firstborn children would die! This event is still celebrated by the people of Israel today. It is called Passover.

In fact, through all these plagues, the Israelites were not touched—not once! Only the Egyptians were affected by the plagues! I'm sure every time Moses obeyed and God acted that Moses became more fearless and his faith grew!

The last plague finally got Pharaoh's attention because even he lost a son! He was finally ready to let the people go.

And the race was on to get out while the getting out was good. Next, one of the most famous stories of the Bible takes place. Do you know what it is? Yes, that's it—the Red Sea parts for the children of Israel to get out of Egypt!

Let's find out what the Bible records about this amazing event and see what we can dig out about Moses' faith!

11. Read Exodus 14:5-31. It's long, but it is surely exciting!

5When the king of Egypt was told that the people had fled, Pharaoh and his servants had a change of heart toward the people, and they said, "What is this we have done, that we have let Israel go from serving us?" **6**So he made his chariot ready and took his people with him; **7**and he took six hundred select chariots, and all the *other* chariots of Egypt with officers over all of them. **8**The LORD hardened the heart of Pharaoh, king of Egypt, and he chased after the sons of Israel as the sons of Israel were going out boldly. **9**Then the Egyptians chased after them *with* all the horses *and* chariots of Pharaoh, his horsemen and his army, and they overtook them camping by the sea, beside Pi-hahiroth, in front of Baal-zephon.

10As Pharaoh drew near, the sons of Israel looked, and behold, the Egyptians were marching after them, and they became very frightened; so the sons of Israel cried out to the LORD. **11**Then they said to Moses, "Is it because there were no graves in Egypt that you have taken us away to die in the wilderness? Why have you dealt with us in this way, bringing us out of Egypt? **12**"Is this not the word that we spoke to you in Egypt, saying, 'Leave us alone that we may serve the Egyptians'? For it would have been better for us to serve the Egyptians than to die in the wilderness."

13But Moses said to the people, "Do not fear! Stand by and see the salvation of the LORD which He will accomplish for you today; for the Egyptians whom you have seen today, you will never see them again forever. **14**"The LORD will fight for you while you keep silent."

15Then the LORD said to Moses, "Why are you crying out to Me? Tell the sons of Israel to go forward. **16**"As for you, lift up your staff and stretch out your hand over the sea and divide it, and the sons of Israel shall go through the midst of the sea on dry land. **17**"As for Me, behold, I will harden the hearts of the Egyptians so that they will go in after them; and I will be honored through Pharaoh and all his army, through his chariots and his horsemen. **18**"Then the Egyptians will know that I am the LORD, when I am honored through Pharaoh, through his chariots and his horsemen."

19The angel of God, who had been going before the camp of Israel, moved and went behind them; and the pillar of cloud moved from before them and stood behind them. **20**So it came between the camp of Egypt and the camp of Israel; and there was the cloud along with the darkness, yet it gave light at night. Thus the one did not come near the other all night.

21Then Moses stretched out his hand over the sea; and the LORD swept the sea *back* by a strong east wind all night and turned the sea into dry land, so the waters were divided. **22**The sons of Israel went through the midst of the sea on the dry land, and the waters *were like* a wall to them on their right hand and on their left. **23**Then the Egyptians took up the pursuit, and all Pharaoh's horses, his chariots and his horsemen went in after them into the midst of the sea. **24**At the morning watch, the LORD looked down on the army of the Egyptians through the pillar of fire and cloud and brought the army of the Egyptians into confusion. **25**He caused their chariot wheels to swerve, and He made them drive with difficulty; so the Egyptians said, "Let us flee from Israel, for the LORD is fighting for them against the Egyptians."

26Then the LORD said to Moses, "Stretch out your hand over the sea so that the waters may come back over the Egyptians, over their chariots and their horsemen." **27**So Moses stretched out his hand over the sea, and the sea returned to its normal state at daybreak, while the Egyptians were fleeing right into it; then the LORD overthrew the Egyptians in the midst of the sea. **28**The waters returned and covered the chariots and the horsemen, even Pharaoh's entire army that had gone into the sea after them; not even one of them remained. **29**But the sons of Israel walked on dry land through the midst of the sea, and the waters *were like* a wall to them on their right hand and on their left.

30Thus the LORD saved Israel that day from the hand of the Egyptians, and Israel saw the Egyptians dead on the seashore. **31**When Israel saw the great power which the LORD had used against the Egyptians, the people feared the LORD, and they believed in the LORD and in His servant Moses. (Exodus 14:5-31)

12. Let's dig in just one verse for now. Look in verse 13. What does Moses say to the people?

This sounds like a man of fearless faith to me!

13. I don't want you to miss a neat treasure. You actually already have it because you discovered it in Dig Eight, but you might forget to examine it again. Do you recall that Joseph's family was the group of people that God had talked to Abraham about? Well, think now. This same group of people is the group that God is having Moses lead out of Egpyt! Awesome!

Can you believe all that God did to convince Pharaoh to let the people go? Moses had to have a fearless faith to keep going back to face this cruel king again and again, didn't he? But his faith was in a God who had proved He could do miracles—and when Moses saw God's power and knew what God wanted to do, Moses was fearless!

LAYER FIVE: Leader of Israelities

Moses was an Israelite who, as a child, had been adopted by Egyptians. He later decided he wanted to live with his people, and he gave up all the riches of Egypt to go back to his people! He became a shepherd. Then, God called him to become a man of fearless faith!

1. Let's dig in our faith hall of fame chapter and see what is recorded there about Moses!

23By faith Moses, when he was born, was hidden for three months by his parents, because they saw he was a beautiful child; and they were not afraid of the king's edict. **24**By faith Moses, when he had grown up, refused to be called the son of Pharaoh's daughter, **25**choosing rather to endure ill-treatment with the people of God than to enjoy the passing pleasures of sin, **26**considering the reproach of Christ greater riches than the treasures of Egypt; for he was looking to the reward. **27**By faith he left Egypt, not fearing the wrath of the king; for he endured, as seeing Him who is unseen. **28**By faith he kept the Passover and the sprinkling of the blood, so that he who destroyed the firstborn would not touch them. **29**By faith they passed through the Red Sea as though *they were passing* through dry land; and the Egyptians, when they attempted it, were drowned. (Hebrews 11:23-29)

2. You see that many of the truths you have already uncovered from other parts of the Bible are repeated here in Hebrews 11. But let's dig a little deeper. Go back and circle the words "by faith" with your green pencil.

3. Fill in the spaces below to see again what Moses' faith enabled him to do.

verse 24: refused to be called _____ _____ ___ _____ _____

verse 27: he left _____

verse 28: kept the _____

verse 29: they passed _____ ___ _____ _____

Moses became a man of fearless faith because he believed and obeyed God. Moses' obedience made him a righteous man. And his fearless faith made him as bold as a lion before Pharaoh!

For years God used Moses to lead the children of Israel toward the promised land—the same land God had told Abraham about. God called Moses up a mountain where He gave him the Ten Commandments. He instructed Moses to build a place in the wilderness, called the tabernacle, where God came to live with the people. God said that He talked with Moses like a man talks with his friend—face to face! In fact, when Moses came down from talking with God, he had to cover his face—it was so bright from seeing God that it blinded the people!

Ask God today to work with you in ways that will strengthen your faith, build your confidence in Him, and make you fearless when it comes to doing what He asks you to do. Ask Him for a faith that will make you as bold as a lion!

When we started to learn about Moses, I told you that he was one of my favorite Bible characters. I also said that I'd tell you why I liked him so much. After God calls Moses to lead His people out of Egypt, Moses tells God that he is not sure he can do a good job because he stammers when he talks. He asks God to give him someone to talk for him. And God does! God has Moses' brother Aaron work with him.

Moses did not let his shortcomings or weaknesses stop him from doing what God asked him to do. He talked with God about how to work things out in spite of the problem. I know some people who give up or who will not try if things are too hard. But I love that Moses did not give up. And I love that something that could have embarrassed him did not stop him! He became fearless in doing what God asked him to do, even though he could not give a great speech every time he had to talk to Pharaoh!

4. Look on page 120 for a fun puzzle to work!

5. Record your "Truth Treasures."

You have been on a long, hard dig! And you deserve a good, long break. Ask your parents to do something extra fun with you. One of my favorite things to do is play miniature golf. I hardly ever get to play since I live a long way from a course, but I think I will play today since I want a nice, long break, too!

See you in Dig Ten soon! I am looking forward to it because I already know what a great story we will dig into!

Truth Treasures for the Week

1.

2.

3.

Bury the Treasure:

The wicked flees when no one is pursuing, but the righteous are as bold as a lion. (Proverbs 28:1)

Truth Trackers: Heroes of Faith

Connect the Dots

There are 221 dots in this puzzle. Connect them to learn the important message that Moses gave to the people of Israel.

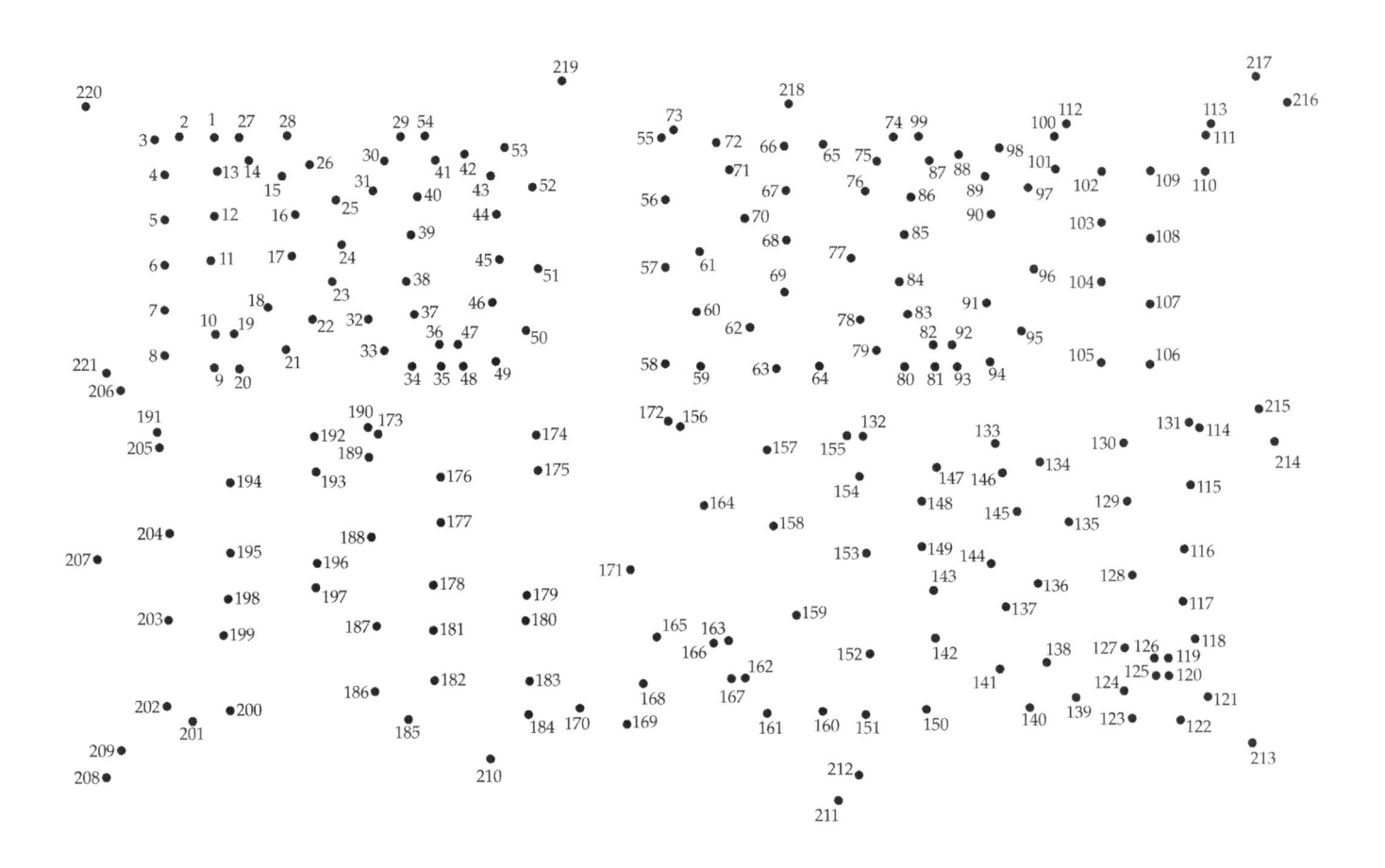

solution on page 167

Dig 10

Rahab's Faith of Abandon

Tools of the Trade

1. Colored pencils
2. Pen or pencil
3. Dictionary
4. Game on page 132

Directions for Diggers

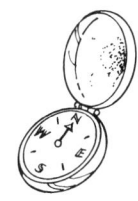

In this dig you will uncover the faith of a woman who did not know God personally. She had heard about Him, and, in the story you will dig through, she comes face to face with two men who were on God's side and knew God.

When you see what she did for these men of God—and what she risked to do it—you will see why we are calling her faith a "faith of abandon."

Don't forget to check in with headquarters. It is very important to understand this faith, and you want to be sure to ask the Holy Spirit to help you find all the truth you can about it.

LAYER ONE: Spies in the City!

The woman whose faith you are digging to uncover is Rahab. She lived in a city called Jericho. Jericho was situated in the middle of a desert land—kind of like where I live. But the amazing thing about Jericho was that, even though it was in a desert, nearby there was a lush area where wonderful fruits and vegetables could grow. It was a beautiful setting for a city!

The men who lived in Jericho built walls around it to protect the people from any intruders who would try to capture the city or attack and steal their possessions. So, Jericho was what we call a "walled city." There were houses built in and on the walls, and Rahab lived in one of these houses.

Let's read some of Rahab's story and begin to dig out facts about her. Also, begin to think about her faith—a faith of abandon.

1. Before we begin to read, maybe you should get your dictionary and look up the word "abandon." I bet you have some idea about what it means, but I want to be sure we are thinking alike about it since it's the word we are using to describe Rahab's faith. Write a short definition below.

I wrote: "Abandon means that someone gives themselves over to something." You may have a hard time understanding my definition, so let me tell you a little about what I wrote.

If you abandon yourself to something, you totally get into it. You do not hold back anything. Some of you may have abandoned yourself to a sport you really like—maybe baseball or biking. Or maybe you are an artist. Others of you may have abandoned yourself to piano or to cooking or to ballet. I hope you get the idea. I know you will see why we are calling Rahab's faith a faith of abandon as we dig.

2. Okay, now let's begin to dig into Rahab's story. It is an amazing one! Read Joshua 2:1-7 and think carefully about each verse as you dig.

1Then Joshua the son of Nun sent two men as spies secretly from Shittim, saying, "Go, view the land, especially Jericho." So they went and came into the house of a harlot whose name was Rahab, and lodged there. **2**It was told the king of Jericho, saying, "Behold, men from the sons of Israel have come here tonight to search out the land." **3**And the king of Jericho sent *word* to Rahab, saying, "Bring out the men who have come to you, who have entered your house, for they have come to search out all the land." **4**But the woman had taken the two men and hidden them, and she said, "Yes, the men came to me, but I did not know where they were from. **5**"It came about when *it was time* to shut the gate at dark, that the men went out; I do not know where the men went. Pursue them quickly, for you will overtake them." **6**But she had brought them up to the roof and hidden them in the stalks of flax which she had laid in order on the roof. **7**So the men pursued them on the road to the Jordan to the fords; and as soon as those who were pursuing them had gone out, they shut the gate. (Joshua 2:1-7)

Rahab's Faith of Abandon

2. Joshua sent two spies to view the land, especially Jericho. When they had completed their mission, where did they stay the night?

3. Who gets word that spies are checking out the land?

4. What does the king do once he knows where the men are?

5. What had Rahab done with the men in verse 4?

6. How does Rahab respond to the question of where the men are in verses 4-5? Remember, she is responding to the king!

7. What does verse 6 tell you about what she had done with these men?

8. Did men from the city believe Rahab's tale of where the men had gone? How do you know?

9. When these men left the city to look for the spies, what happened to the gate of the city?

10. Now the gate is closed to the city. Where are the spies at this point?

So, Rahab had taken in two spies and then hidden them—even from the king's men, who had been sent to tell her to give up the spies. Can you imagine what might have happened if the king found out she was hiding these men?

Can you imagine why she hid the men? She must have had a very good reason, don't you think? Remember, too, that the king's men have gone to look for the spies and now they are locked inside the city—on Rahab's roof!

This is such an exciting story. I bet you want to keep digging to see what happens, but you have worked long and hard. It is time for a break. Enjoy yourself, and I will see you in Layer Two soon!

LAYER TWO: Trusting a Spy?

Let's not waste one moment! Let's dig!

1. Continue to dig through the account of Rahab and the spies. Read Joshua 2:8-13.

⁸Now before they lay down, she came up to them on the roof, ⁹and said to the men, "I know that the LORD has given you the land, and that the terror of you has fallen on us, and that all the inhabitants of the land have melted away before you. ¹⁰"For we have heard how the LORD dried up the water of the Red Sea before you when you came out of Egypt, and what you did to the two kings of the Amorites who were beyond the Jordan, to Sihon and Og, whom you utterly destroyed. ¹¹"When we heard *it*, our hearts melted and no courage remained in any man any longer because of you; for the LORD your God, He is God in heaven above and on earth beneath. ¹²"Now therefore, please swear to me by the LORD, since I have dealt kindly with you, that you also will deal kindly with my father's household, and give me a pledge of truth, ¹³and spare my father and my mother and my brothers and my sisters, with all who belong to them, and deliver our lives from death." (Joshua 2:8-13)

2. First, you see Rahab go to the roof where the spies are hiding. She has something to say to them before she helps them any further. I think what Rahab says is awesome! Let's take a treasure at a time and examine it.

In verse 9 she says three things that she believes are true. List those below.

Rahab says, "I know

that the _____ _____ _____ _____ _____ _____

Rahab's Faith of Abandon

that the _____ ____ _____ _____ _____ ____ ____

that all the inhabitants of the _____ ____ _____ _____ _____ ____

Can you see that Rahab has some idea that God is going to allow the city of Jericho to be conquered by these men and their army? She believes this for a good reason. Let's keep digging!

3. Read verse 10 again. One of the stories Rahab heard is one you should recognize too. What is it?

Yes, you uncovered the treasure of how God parted the Red Sea when you looked at Moses' faith. The stories of what God was doing for His people were spreading far and wide, and Rahab had heard of this God, too!

4. What does Rahab say happened when she and others heard of what God was doing for His people? She says two things. Write them both below.

5. Then, in the same verse where she says that their hearts melted and their courage failed, she makes an amazing statement about God. Write below what she says about Him.

Rahab had heard of the mighty acts of God, and she believed that He was indeed God. She even says that He is God of heaven above and earth beneath. She says, basically, that He is God of everything. She sounds convinced to me! And we are about to see what kind of faith she has!

6. Read verses 12-13 again and see what Rahab asks. Write what you find.

    Yes, Rahab knew the army of God's people was coming against Jericho. And she knew that God was acting for His people. Think now about the kind of faith it took for her to ask these two men of God to save her and her family!

    Rahab did not know a lot about God. As far as we know, no one had ever talked with her about who He was and what He would want her to do. She had only heard stories! But she had come to believe that God was truly God, and in this moment she gave all of herself over to this belief.

    She risked everything to help these men, even before she asked them for help. She did not hold on to her safety and went against the king's request to give the men over. Also, she did not try to figure out a way for the men to save her and her family—she just asked to be saved! She gave over all her thoughts and ideas to these men God had sent to spy out the land, and she believed the God they knew could save her!

Rahab abandoned herself to the men who were on God's mission—and to the God she believed was working on their behalf. Let's see what God does in return. Can you wait? Well, we'll keep digging as soon as you get to Layer Three.

LAYER THREE: A Deal with Spies?

1. Let's dig and see what the spies say to Rahab's request. Read Joshua 2:14-21.

¹⁴So the men said to her, "Our life for yours if you do not tell this business of ours; and it shall come about when the LORD gives us the land that we will deal kindly and faithfully with you."

¹⁵Then she let them down by a rope through the window, for her house was on the city wall, so that she was living on the wall. ¹⁶She said to them, "Go to the hill country, so that the pursuers will not happen upon you, and hide yourselves there for three days until the pursuers return. Then afterward you may go on your way." ¹⁷The men said to her, "We *shall be* free from this oath to you which you have made us swear, ¹⁸unless, when we come into the land, you tie this cord of scarlet thread in the window through which you let us down, and gather to yourself into the house your father and your mother and your brothers and all your father's household. ¹⁹"It shall come about that anyone who goes out of the doors of your house into the street, his blood *shall be* on his own head, and we *shall be* free; but anyone who is with you in the house, his blood *shall be* on our head if a hand is *laid* on him. ²⁰"But if you tell this business of ours, then we shall be free from the oath which you have made us swear." ²¹She said, "According to your words, so be it." So she sent them away, and they departed; and she tied the scarlet cord in the window. (Joshua 2:14-21)

Rahab's Faith of Abandon

2. Do the men agree to spare Rahab and her family? What exactly do they say about her request in verse 14?

3. After the deal is stuck, Rahab gets the men out of town. How does she do it? Look in verse 15.

4. Where does she tell them to hide?

5. How long does she tell them to stay in hiding?

6. The men have a couple of instructions for Rahab before they go. First, they tell her to hang something in her window so that they will be able to identify the house when the battle begins. What was it?

7. They also tell her to gather all of her family into her house. What do they say will happen if anyone goes outside after the battle begins?

8. In verse 20 what do the men say will happen if Rahab discusses any of their plans with someone else?

9. How does Rahab respond to the men telling her she cannot talk about the plan? First, what does she say?

10. Then what does she do?

11. The men follow her instructions to hide for three days. Then they return to Joshua, who had sent them to spy out the land. Do they give a good report? Do they say that the land can be conquered? Read verses 22-24 and write your answer.

²²They departed and came to the hill country, and remained there for three days until the pursuers returned. Now the pursuers had sought *them* all along the road, but had not found *them*. ²³Then the two men returned and came down from the hill country and crossed over and came to Joshua the son of Nun, and they related to him all that had happened to them. ²⁴They said to Joshua, "Surely the LORD has given all the land into our hands; moreover, all the inhabitants of the land have melted away before us." (Joshua 2:22-24)

So far, Rahab's faith seems to be paying off, doesn't it? We'll dig into what happens next in Layer Four. In the meantime, think about what Rahab said about God—when she had only heard about Him and had not even met any of His people!

> Do you have the kind of faith Rahab had? Can you abandon everything to God even though you have not see Him? I know you have met people who know God and who serve Him, so you have more than Rahab had! Can you give yourself over to God and what He wants to do for you?
> Think hard about that, and talk to your parents tonight about it.

LAYER FOUR: The Spies Bring an Army

Today we will dig into the story about the battle of the people of God against the city of Jericho. Once you begin to dig, you may realize that you already know a lot of the story. Here we go!

1. Read Joshua 6:1-5.

¹Now Jericho was tightly shut because of the sons of Israel; no one went out and no one came in. ²The LORD said to Joshua, "See, I have given Jericho into your hand, with its king *and* the valiant warriors. ³"You shall march around the city, all the men of war circling the city once. You shall do so for six days. ⁴"Also seven priests shall carry seven trumpets of rams' horns before the ark; then on the seventh day you shall march around the city seven times, and the priests shall blow the trumpets. ⁵"It shall be that when they make a long blast with the ram's horn, and when you hear the sound of the trumpet, all the people shall shout with a great shout; and the wall of the city will fall down flat, and the people will go up every man straight ahead." (Joshua 6:1-5)

Rahab's Faith of Abandon

2. What is happening in Jericho?

3. Why is the city closed so tightly?

4. In verses 2-5, the Lord, God, gives instructions about how to go about the battle. Read these verses again.

5. Joshua then gives the people instructions about the battle. He also gives instructions about Rahab's house. Let's dig and see what he says.

17"The city shall be under the ban, it and all that is in it belongs to the LORD; only Rahab the harlot and all who are with her in the house shall live, because she hid the messengers whom we sent. 18"But as for you, only keep yourselves from the things under the ban, so that you do not covet them and take some of the things under the ban, and make the camp of Israel accursed and bring trouble on it. 19"But all the silver and gold and articles of bronze and iron are holy to the LORD; they shall go into the treasury of the LORD." (Joshua 6:17-19)

6. Who does Joshua say will be allowed to live?

7. Why does he say she is going to be allowed to live?

Can you see that God is honoring Rahab's faith? She acted on faith and hid the spies because of who she believed God was—and God did what the spies promised!

8. Dig and see what happened at the end of the battle.

20So the people shouted, and priests blew the trumpets; and when the people heard the sound of the trumpet, the people shouted with a great shout and the wall fell down flat, so that the people went up into the city, every man straight ahead, and they took the city. 21They utterly destroyed everything in the city, both man and woman, young and old, and ox and sheep and donkey, with the edge of the sword. (Joshua 6:20-21)

9. Did the walls fall?

10. Did they destroy everything?

11. But don't forget about Rahab and her family. See what Joshua says about her.

²²Joshua said to the two men who had spied out the land, "Go into the harlot's house and bring the woman and all she has out of there, as you have sworn to her." ²³So the young men who were spies went in and brought out Rahab and her father and her mother and her brothers and all she had; they also brought out all her relatives and placed them outside the camp of Israel. (Joshua 6:22-23)

12. See what happened to the city next.

They burned the city with fire, and all that was in it. Only the silver and gold, and articles of bronze and iron, they put into the treasury of the house of the LORD. (Joshua 6:24)

13. And again see what happened to Rahab and her family as the city burned! Write what you see.

However, Rahab the harlot and her father's household and all she had, Joshua spared; and she has lived in the midst of Israel to this day, for she hid the messengers whom Joshua sent to spy out Jericho. (Joshua 6:25)

Meet me in Layer Five as soon as you can. I am eager to get to the bottom of this dig because it has been so great!

LAYER FIVE: The Reward of Faith

1. Let's see what the faith hall of fame says about Rahab.

By faith Rahab the harlot did not perish along with those who were disobedient, after she had welcomed the spies in peace. (Hebrews 11:31)

Rahab's Faith of Abandon

2. What do you find out about the people in Jericho in this verse?

Yes, the Bible says they were disobedient.

3. What does this verse say Rahab did?

Yes, she welcomed the spies in peace. She welcomed these men of God in peace because, in faith, she had abandoned herself to what she believed about God. She had heard about Him and decided that He was the God of heaven and earth! She abandoned herself to Him and believed He would save her and her family!

4. Have some fun now with the puzzle on page 132.

5. And don't forget your "Truth Treasures."

You have come to the bottom of Dig Ten! Amazing, isn't it? You are doing such a great job of digging out truth! I hope you won't just put it aside after you look at it. I hope you will continue to pick it up, look at it, think about it, and decide what you will do about your faith as a result of these truths you have discovered!

Truth Treasures for the Week

1.

2.

3.

Bury the Treasure:

For God so loved the world, that He gave His only begotten Son, that whoever believes in Him shall not perish, but have eternal life. (John 3:16)

Rahab's Lifeline

Rahab lowered a rope through her window to help the spies escape, but Rahab had her own lifeline through her faith in God. To discover what Rahab believed that saved her life and the lives of her family, unravel the rope of this puzzle. Color every third twist of rope, then use those letters to fill in the blanks at the bottom of the page. The first ones have been done for you.

"... T H E   L O R D   Y O U R   G O D ,   H E   I S   G O D   I N   H E A V E N   A B O V E ,   A N D   I N   E A R T H   B E N E A T H ."

(Joshua 2:11)

solution on page 167

Dig 11

David's Patient Faith

Tools of the Trade

1. Colored pencils
2. Pen or pencil
3. Game on page 146

Directions for Diggers

I bet you know about the man whose faith we will examine in this dig! David was a shepherd boy who became the great king of Israel! God was interested in David for one specific reason, and you will find that reason as you dig. I think you will see that this reason is also what enabled David to become a man of patient faith.

Patient faith believes what God says and is willing to wait for God to do what He promised. This faith does not take matters into its own hands. It does not run ahead of God and try to make things happen. It is a faith that is convinced God can do exactly what He has said—and it is sure He will do it in His time and in His way!

As you prepare your tools for this dig, don't forget to check in with headquarters. I think you are really going to have a great time on this dig!

LAYER ONE: The Giant Slayer

I am certain that you know the story of David and Goliath. Do you recall that this giant of a man teased the army of God day after day by calling to them to send a man to fight him?

That may not seem like such a big deal, but when you think about the fact that Goliath was over nine feet tall, it helps you see why no one was rushing forward to challenge him!

David shows up on the scene because his father sent him to the front of the battle to take food for his brothers. Let's see what happens. It is a long story, but you will dig through it quickly because it is so exciting!

³³Then Saul said to David, "You are not able to go against this Philistine to fight with him; for you are *but* a youth while he has been a warrior from his youth." ³⁴But David said to Saul, "Your servant was tending his father's sheep. When a lion or a bear came and took a lamb from the flock, ³⁵I went out after him and attacked him, and rescued *it* from his mouth; and when he rose up against me, I seized *him* by his beard and struck him and killed him. ³⁶"Your servant has killed both the lion and the bear; and this uncircumcised Philistine will be like one of them, since he has taunted the armies of the living God." ³⁷And David said, "The LORD who delivered me from the paw of the lion and from the paw of the bear, He will deliver me from the hand of this Philistine." And Saul said to David, "Go, and may the LORD be with you." ³⁸Then Saul clothed David with his garments and put a bronze helmet on his head, and he clothed him with armor. ³⁹David girded his sword over his armor and tried to walk, for he had not tested *them*. So David said to Saul, "I cannot go with these, for I have not tested *them*." And David took them off. ⁴⁰He took his stick in his hand and chose for himself five smooth stones from the brook, and put them in the shepherd's bag which he had, even in *his* pouch, and his sling was in his hand; and he approached the Philistine.

⁴¹Then the Philistine came on and approached David, with the shield-bearer in front of him. ⁴²When the Philistine looked and saw David, he disdained him; for he was *but* a youth, and ruddy, with a handsome appearance. ⁴³The Philistine said to David, "Am I a dog, that you come to me with sticks?" And the Philistine cursed David by his gods. ⁴⁴The Philistine also said to David, "Come to me, and I will give your flesh to the birds of the sky and the beasts of the field." ⁴⁵Then David said to the Philistine, "You come to me with a sword, a spear, and a javelin, but I come to you in the name of the LORD of hosts, the God of the armies of Israel, whom you have taunted. ⁴⁶"This day the LORD will deliver you up into my hands, and I will strike you down and remove your head from you. And I will give the dead bodies of the army of the Philistines this day to the birds of the sky and the wild beasts of the earth, that all the earth may know that there is a God in Israel, ⁴⁷and that all this assembly may know that the LORD does not deliver by sword or by spear; for the battle is the LORD's and He will give you into our hands." (1 Samuel 17:33-47)

David's Patient Faith

1. You see that David seems to have no fear! What does he say to Saul about how prepared he is to fight this giant? Look at verses 34-35 again to see what he says. Write why David feels ready to take on Goliath.

2. In verse 36, what does David say Goliath has done?

3. Then in verse 37, what does David say God will do?

4. Saul dresses David in his own personal armor, but it is too big and heavy for David. So, in the end, what does David have with him when he goes to fight the giant? Look at what verse 40 says.

5. How does David tell Goliath he is coming against him in verse 45?

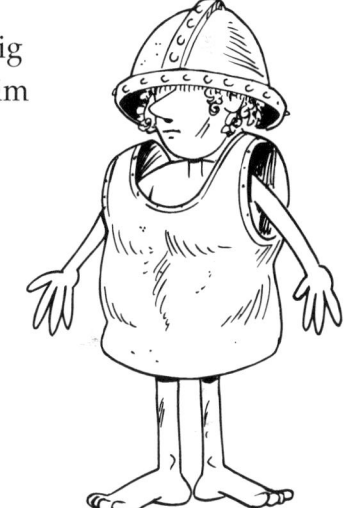

6. Now read the rest of the story.

⁴⁸Then it happened when the Philistine rose and came and drew near to meet David, that David ran quickly toward the battle line to meet the Philistine. ⁴⁹And David put his hand into his bag and took from it a stone and slung *it*, and struck the Philistine on his forehead. And the stone sank into his forehead, so that he fell on his face to the ground.
 ⁵⁰Thus David prevailed over the Philistine with a sling and a stone, and he struck the Philistine and killed him; but there was no sword in David's hand. ⁵¹Then David ran and stood over the Philistine and took his sword and drew it out of its sheath and killed him, and cut off his head with it. When the Philistines saw that their champion was dead, they fled. (1 Samuel 17:48-51)

David won the battle! Think again about what God said about David. God was interested in David's heart! And in this story you see that in David's heart he trusted God to protect him, and he was concerned about God's honor. He did not want this man who was making fun of God to get away with it. And God then honored David's heart—He enabled him to win the battle!

LAYER TWO: The Shepherd Boy

Even before we worked through Layer One, you probably remembered David was a shepherd boy who watched his dad's flocks. Did you also remember that he was the youngest of eight brothers? And it was this youngest son that God had in mind when He sent the prophet Samuel to anoint a king for Israel.

At the time that Samuel was sent to anoint David as king over Israel, Saul was already the king. But because Saul was disobedient to the Lord, God rejected him as king and was going to prepare David to take his place. Let's catch up with Samuel and see what is happening.

1. Read 1 Samuel 16:1-5 so you can see for yourself what I just explained to you.

1Now the LORD said to Samuel, "How long will you grieve over Saul, since I have rejected him from being king over Israel? Fill your horn with oil and go; I will send you to Jesse the Bethlehemite, for I have selected a king for Myself among his sons." **2**But Samuel said, "How can I go? When Saul hears *of it*, he will kill me." And the LORD said, "Take a heifer with you and say, 'I have come to sacrifice to the LORD.' **3**"You shall invite Jesse to the sacrifice, and I will show you what you shall do; and you shall anoint for Me the one whom I designate to you." **4**So Samuel did what the LORD said, and came to Bethlehem. And the elders of the city came trembling to meet him and said, "Do you come in peace?" **5**He said, "In peace; I have come to sacrifice to the LORD. Consecrate yourselves and come with me to the sacrifice." He also consecrated Jesse and his sons and invited them to the sacrifice. (1 Samuel 16:1-5)

2. Now read further in the story and see what happens when Samuel sees David's oldest brother.

6When they entered, he looked at Eliab and thought, "Surely the LORD's anointed is before Him." **7**But the LORD said to Samuel, "Do not look at his appearance or at the height of his stature, because I have rejected him; for God *sees* not as man sees, for man looks at the outward appearance, but the LORD looks at the heart." (1 Samuel 16:6-7)

3. Because Eliab is tall and handsome and looks like the kind of man who could be a king, Samuel thinks he has found the man he was sent to anoint. But what does God say to him about appearances? What does God say that He looks at?

David's Patient Faith

That is pretty exciting to me! I know people often think if you are tall or pretty or smart that you are more special than someone else. But aren't you glad to know that God is only interested in your heart and how you respond to Him?

4. One by one the brothers come before Samuel at their father's instruction. But none of these young men is the one God has in mind. Read and see how Jesse, David's father, brought all his older sons to be considered and how, in the end, he sent for David.

8Then Jesse called Abinadab and made him pass before Samuel. And he said, "The LORD has not chosen this one either." 9Next Jesse made Shammah pass by. And he said, 'The LORD has not chosen this one either." 10Thus Jesse made seven of his sons pass before Samuel. But Samuel said to Jesse, "The LORD has not chosen these." 11And Samuel said to Jesse, "Are these all the children?" And he said, "There remains yet the youngest, and behold, he is tending the sheep." Then Samuel said to Jesse, "Send and bring him; for we will not sit down until he comes here."
12So he sent and brought him in. Now he was ruddy, with beautiful eyes and a handsome appearance. And the LORD said, "Arise, anoint him; for this is he."
(1 Samuel 16:8-12)

5. What happens to David after Samuel anoints him? Read below to see.

Then Samuel took the horn of oil and anointed him in the midst of his brothers; and the Spirit of the LORD came mightily upon David from that day forward. And Samuel arose and went to Ramah. (1 Samuel 16:13)

6. Now look at 1 Samuel 16:14 to see what happened to Saul, the king.

Now the Spirit of the LORD departed from Saul, and an evil spirit from the LORD terrorized him. (1 Samuel 16:14)

7. Then an amazing thing happens: One of the men who works for Saul suggests that he was being bothered by an evil spirit. He also suggests that Saul find someone who could play the harp so that, when Saul felt bad because of the spirit, the music would soothe him.

Guess what another one of Saul's servants suggests? It is hard to believe, but he suggests that they send for David! I am sure David had learned to play as he sat alone in the fields watching the sheep. They send for David, and his father, Jesse, packs him up and sends him to Saul. David enters the service of the king!

Read the Bible's account of these events so you can see for yourself how David came to work for Saul!

14Now the Spirit of the LORD departed from Saul, and an evil spirit from the LORD terrorized him. **15**Saul's servants then said to him, "Behold now, an evil spirit from God is terrorizing you. **16**"Let our lord now command your servants who are before you. Let them seek a man who is a skillful player on the harp; and it shall come about when the evil spirit from God is on you, that he shall play *the harp* with his hand, and you will be well." **17**So Saul said to his servants, "Provide for me now a man who can play well and bring *him* to me." **18**Then one of the young men said, "Behold, I have seen a son of Jesse the Bethlehemite who is a skillful musician, a mighty man of valor, a warrior, one prudent in speech, and a handsome man; and the LORD is with him." **19**So Saul sent messengers to Jesse and said, "Send me your son David who is with the flock." **20**Jesse took a donkey *loaded with* bread and a jug of wine and a young goat, and sent *them* to Saul by David his son. **21**Then David came to Saul and attended him; and Saul loved him greatly, and he became his armor bearer. **22**Saul sent to Jesse, saying, "Let David now stand before me, for he has found favor in my sight." **23**So it came about whenever the *evil* spirit from God came to Saul, David would take the harp and play *it* with his hand; and Saul would be refreshed and be well, and the evil spirit would depart from him. (1 Samuel 16:14-23)

Well, you have seen in this layer how David went from being a shepherd to being anointed as the future king of Israel. And you also see how he moved from the rocky, lonely fields with the sheep into the palace of the current king and became his armor bearer! Two pretty big moves!

Don't forget the treasure you discovered—that God looks at the heart. Hold on to that one and look carefully at it. Later you will see why we are looking at it so carefully!

I will see you soon. I am going for a nice long walk to think about who David was and who he was becoming! See you in Layer Three.

LAYER THREE: The Warrior

David is a hero now! The people are thrilled with him, and often they sing songs about how brave he is! Let's see what is happening with Saul since David has become so popular.

David's Patient Faith

1. Read 1 Samuel 18:5-9.

⁵So David went out wherever Saul sent him, *and* prospered; and Saul set him over the men of war. And it was pleasing in the sight of all the people and also in the sight of Saul's servants.

⁶It happened as they were coming, when David returned from killing the Philistine, that the women came out of all the cities of Israel, singing and dancing, to meet King Saul, with tambourines, with joy and with musical instruments. ⁷The women sang as they played, and said,

"Saul has slain his thousands,

And David his ten thousands."

⁸Then Saul became very angry, for this saying displeased him; and he said, "They have ascribed to David ten thousands, but to me they have ascribed thousands. Now what more can he have but the kingdom?" ⁹Saul looked at David with suspicion from that day on. (1 Samuel 18:5-9)

2. David did everything Saul asked him to do—and he did it well. What did Saul do in return?

3. Look in verse 6 to see what the women did when the men returned from battle. Write what you uncover.

4. Why did the song upset Saul? You will see what he said in verse 8.

5. What does verse 9 say that Saul did from that time on?

That's right. David continues to do well, and since so many people are excited about him and are giving him credit for killing many in battle, Saul is jealous.

I think you will be very surprised to see what David does as you dig in Layer Four. I will be there waiting when you are ready!

LAYER FOUR: The Future King's Heart

Remember, David secretly has been anointed to become king of Israel. Saul is still the king, but God is displeased with Saul and God's spirit is not with him now. David has killed Goliath and also is becoming a hero in battle. David is growing in popularity with the people, too. Saul is jealous and watching David carefully.

Remember, too, that God is impressed with David's heart. God knows that David wants to do the right thing—he wants to do what God wants him to do.

Think about the fact that David knows he will be the king. He also knows the people are not very happy with Saul. What would you do if you were David and you had a chance to get Saul out of the picture? Let's see what David did.

1. Read 1 Samuel 24:1-8. Dig carefully so you can answer some questions!

1Now when Saul returned from pursuing the Philistines, he was told, saying, "Behold, David is in the wilderness of Engedi." **2**Then Saul took three thousand chosen men from all Israel and went to seek David and his men in front of the Rocks of the Wild Goats. **3**He came to the sheepfolds on the way, where there *was* a cave; and Saul went in to relieve himself. Now David and his men were sitting in the inner recesses of the cave. **4**The men of David said to him, "Behold, *this is* the day of which the Lord said to you, 'Behold; I am about to give your enemy into your hand, and you shall do to him as it seems good to you.'" Then David arose and cut off the edge of Saul's robe secretly. **5**It came about afterward that David's conscience bothered him because he had cut off the edge of Saul's *robe.* **6**So he said to his men, "Far be it from me because of the Lord that I should do this thing to my lord, the Lord's anointed, to stretch out my hand against him, since he is the Lord's anointed." **7**David persuaded his men with *these* words and did not allow them to rise up against Saul. And Saul arose, left the cave, and went on *his* way.

David's Patient Faith

⁸Now afterward David arose and went out of the cave and called after Saul, saying, "My lord the king!" And when Saul looked behind him, David bowed with his face to the ground and prostrated himself. (1 Samuel 24:1-8)

2. David called Saul "the Lord's anointed" in verse 6. David will not harm Saul because he knows that God chose Saul to reign. And David knows that when God wants Saul out of office—and David in office—that God will take care of the situation.

3. Look in the next verses to see what David said to Saul outside the cave. Write in your own words what he said.

⁹David said to Saul, "Why do you listen to the words of men, saying, 'Behold, David seeks to harm you'? ¹⁰"Behold, this day your eyes have seen that the LORD had given you today into my hand in the cave, and some said to kill you, but *my eye* had pity on you; and I said, 'I will not stretch out my hand against my lord, for he is the LORD's anointed.' ¹¹"Now, my father, see! Indeed, see the edge of your robe in my hand! For in that I cut off the edge of your robe and did not kill you, know and perceive that there is no evil or rebellion in my hands, and I have not sinned against you, though you are lying in wait for my life to take it. ¹²"May the LORD judge between you and me, and may the LORD avenge me on you; but my hand shall not be against you. (1 Samuel 24:9-12)

4. What does David say in verse 12 about whether he will hurt Saul?

5. On another day, David again has a chance to take Saul's life so that he can take the throne. Let's look quickly at what happens then. Read 1 Samuel 26:7-17.

⁷So David and Abishai came to the people by night, and behold, Saul lay sleeping inside the circle of the camp with his spear stuck in the ground at his head; and Abner and the people were lying around him. ⁸Then Abishai said to David, "Today God has delivered your enemy into your hand; now therefore, please let me strike him with the spear to the ground with one stroke, and I will not strike him the second time." ⁹But David said to

Abishai, "Do not destroy him, for who can stretch out his hand against the LORD's anointed and be without guilt?" **10**David also said, "As the LORD lives, surely the LORD will strike him, or his day will come that he dies, or he will go down into battle and perish. **11**"The LORD forbid that I should stretch out my hand against the LORD's anointed; but now please take the spear that is at his head and the jug of water, and let us go." **12**So David took the spear and the jug of water from *beside* Saul's head, and they went away, but no one saw or knew *it,* nor did any awake, for they were all asleep, because a sound sleep from the LORD had fallen on them.

13Then David crossed over to the other side and stood on top of the mountain at a distance *with* a large area between them. **14**David called to the people and to Abner the son of Ner, saying, "Will you not answer, Abner?" Then Abner replied, "Who are you who calls to the king?" **15**So David said to Abner, "Are you not a man? And who is like you in Israel? Why then have you not guarded your lord the king? For one of the people came to destroy the king your lord. **16**"This thing that you have done is not good. As the LORD lives, *all* of you must surely die, because you did not guard your lord, the LORD's anointed. And now, see where the king's spear is and the jug of water that was at his head."

17Then Saul recognized David's voice and said, "Is this your voice, my son David?" And David said, "It is my voice, my lord the king." (1 Samuel 26:7-17)

6. David had another good chance to kill Saul, but what does he say in verse 9?

Again, David will not harm the man God put into office. I hope you are beginning to see David's patient faith. He knows he is to become king when Saul is gone, but he is waiting for God to act.

7. Read verse 10 again and write below what David says.

David is willing to wait patiently for God to do what He wants with Saul. David just keeps doing what he is suppose to do and, in faith, patiently trusts God to do the rest!

Think about a faith that is patient. Ask God to give you a heart that will trust Him to do what concerns you in His time and in His way. Pray that you will have a heart like David's—a heart that wants to do all God asks and is willing to wait for His timing.

David's Patient Faith

LAYER FIVE: The Reward of Patient Faith

1. Read 1 Samuel 31:1-6 to see how Saul dies.

1Now the Philistines were fighting against Israel, and the men of Israel fled from before the Philistines and fell slain on Mount Gilboa. **2**The Philistines overtook Saul and his sons; and the Philistines killed Jonathan and Abinadab and Malchi-shua the sons of Saul. **3**The battle went heavily against Saul, and the archers hit him; and he was badly wounded by the archers. **4**Then Saul said to his armor bearer, "Draw your sword and pierce me through with it, otherwise these uncircumcised will come and pierce me through and make sport of me." But his armor bearer would not, for he was greatly afraid. So Saul took his sword and fell on it. **5**When his armor bearer saw that Saul was dead, he also fell on his sword and died with him. **6**Thus Saul died with his three sons, his armor bearer, and all his men on that day together. (1 Samuel 31:1-6)

2. Read 2 Samuel 1:11 to see how David reacted to the news of Saul's death. Write what you uncover.

Then David took hold of his clothes and tore them, and so also did all the men who were with him. (2 Samuel 1:11)

3. Read 2 Samuel 5:4 and write what happens.

David was thirty years old when he became king, and he reigned forty years. (2 Samuel 5:4)

David's faith is rewarded! God did what He said he would do. It took years, but God had a patient faith. And David had a patient heart as he waited on God!

4. In Acts you can uncover a very rich treasure about David. Read Acts 13:21-22 and see what God says about David. Write it below.

21"Then they asked for a king, and God gave them Saul the son of Kish, a man of the tribe of Benjamin, for forty years. **22**"After He had removed him, He raised up David to be their king, concerning whom He also testified and said, 'I have found David the son of Jesse, a man after My heart, who will do all My will.' (Acts 13:21-22) a man after ____ _____, _____ _____ ___ ____ ___ _____

Wouldn't you like God to say that you had a heart that would do all that His heart wanted! WOW! These are the things God said about this man with a patient faith and a godly heart!

Remember that I told you as you began this dig that God was interested in David for one specific reason? Now that you have dug through David's story, can you see what God was interested in? Yes, David's heart!

David's heart trusted God and was willing to wait for God to do what He promised. As you get to know more about God and understand more about how He works, I pray you will become a man or woman with a patient and obedient heart! God loves that!

5. Look at what is recorded about David in the faith hall of fame in verses 32-34. He is listed along with several others. The details of what he did are not there, but his name is among those whom God honored. And by reading all that we have in 1 and 2 Samuel, you know why David is listed in Hebrews 11.

³²And what more shall I say? For time will fail me if I tell of Gideon, Barak, Samson, Jephthah, of David and Samuel and the prophets, ³³who by faith conquered kingdoms, performed *acts of* righteousness, obtained promises, shut the mouths of lions, ³⁴quenched the power of fire, escaped the edge of the sword, from weakness were made strong, became mighty in war, put foreign armies to flight. (Hebrews 11:32-34)

6. There is a very fun puzzle for you on page 146. Don't forget to work it today!

7. Note your three "Truth Treasures."

You have done a great job, and I am most proud of you! I hope you have a nice break and enjoy something fun. I will be ready to begin our last dig when you are ready. Let me know!

Truth Treasures for the Week

1.

2.

3.

BURY THE TREASURE:

Create in me a clean heart, O God, and renew a steadfast spirit within me. (Psalm 51:10)

(This is a verse that David wrote one time after he had sinned. He knew he was wrong, and he is asking God to cleanse his heart and to renew the steadfast or patient spirit he had always had!)

Search and Decipher 2

Truth Trackers: Heroes of Faith

In the following word hunt, find the names of the following ten people and places that we learned about in the story of David. (HINT: This is just like the puzzle from Chapter 1, except that in this case the words are all hidden diagonally.)

David	**Philistine**	**Samuel**	**Eliab**	**Abishai**
Goliath	**Saul**	**Jesse**	**Abner**	**Israel**

After you've circled all the words, place the remaining, uncircled letters on the spaces at the bottom of the page, starting at the arrow and moving from left to right to the bottom. Once you've transferred all the letters, the message will tell you something God said about David.

```
→  P  H  A  A  E  E  V  I  E  F
   O  H  U  B  S  L  A  N  D  L
   D  A  I  S  N  H  I  V  E  I
   D  A  E  L  S  E  H  A  M  A
   D  J  U  I  I  T  R  N  B  L
   A  A  B  F  A  S  T  E  E  R
   S  A  V  I  I  M  T  U  Y  H
   E  A  L  I  R  T  M  I  W  H
   O  O  W  I  D  A  L  L  N  D
   G  O  M  Y  S  W  I  L  L  E
```

"I _ … _,"
_ _ _ _ _ _ … _ _ _ _ _ _ _ _ _ _ _.

(Acts 13:22)

solution on page 168

Dig 12

Jesus: Author and Perfecter of OUR Faith

Tools of the Trade

1. Colored pencils
2. Pen or pencil
3. Dictionary
4. Game on page 158

Directions for Diggers

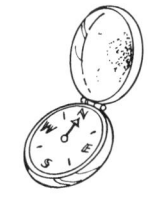

Well, you have seem some amazing examples of men and women who lived their lives in faith. They believed that God was able to do what He said He would do, and they did what He asked them to do, too!

In this last dig—I can't believe it is the last dig!—you are going to sort through the first three verses of Hebrews 12. These verses hold the treasure that will help you understand how you, too, can live your life with the same kind of faith that Abel, Enoch, Sarah, Abraham, Noah, David, Moses, Rahab, Joseph, and others did! I know you want to become a man or woman of amazing faith!

So, grab your gear, and let's head out for our last dig together!

Truth Trackers: Heroes of Faith

LAYER ONE: Let Us...

We are going to dig in only one verse of Hebrews 12 today. You are going to see that you are in a race when you read this verse! As you read, think about what kind of race it may be! Let's start digging because what you are going to find is awesome!

1. Read Hebrews 12:1 very carefully. With your blue pencil, circle the words "let us." These words will show you two things you are told to do.

> Therefore, since we have so great a cloud of witnesses surrounding us, let us also lay aside every encumbrance and the sin which so easily entangles us, and let us run with endurance the race that is set before us. (Hebrews 12:1)

2. Okay, did you discover the two things you are to do? You should have circled the words "let us" two different times. These words are your clue. What are the two things you are to do? Write them below.

3. Do you know what an "encumbrance" is? Look up the word and write a short definition.

Now you see, don't you? An encumbrance is anything that will hold you back. Think about trying to run a race with a fifty-pound sack of potatoes strapped to your back. That would slow you up, wouldn't it? Yes! It would definitely be an encumbrance!

And you probably already know the definition of sin. A simple one—the one the Bible gives us in the book of Isaiah—is that sin is acting apart from what God wants you to do.

4. Now, read verse 1 again and see why you are told to lay aside encumbrances and sin. Who is surrounding you as you run the race?

Jesus: Author and Perfecter of OUR Faith

5. Who do you think this "cloud of witnesses" could be?

Well, if you think that the witnesses are the men and women whose stories you have been digging through, you are right! But let's look at some other verses to see who else may be in the cloud!

6. Go back and read the end of Hebrews 11. We will start digging right after the part that talks about Rahab. So, let's start digging in verse 32.

> **32**And what more shall I say? For time will fail me if I tell of Gideon, Barak, Samson, Jephthah, of David and Samuel and the prophets, **33**who by faith conquered kingdoms, performed *acts of* righteousness, obtained promises, shut the mouths of lions, **34**quenched the power of fire, escaped the edge of the sword, from weakness were made strong, became mighty in war, put foreign armies to flight. **35**Women received *back* their dead by resurrection; and others were tortured, not accepting their release, so that they might obtain a better resurrection; **36**and others experienced mockings and scourgings, yes, also chains and imprisonment. **37**They were stoned, they were sawn in two, they were tempted, they were put to death with the sword; they went about in sheepskins, in goatskins, being destitute, afflicted, ill-treated **38**(*men of* whom the world was not worthy), wandering in deserts and mountains and caves and holes in the ground.
>
> **39**And all these…gained approval through their faith…. (Hebrews 11:32-39a)

4. Aren't you amazed by some of the things you read? These are things that happened to men and women because of their faith! These men and women did what God asked them to do—no matter what. And, remember, God rewarded them!

You discovered in this layer that men and women who lived by faith long ago are now a cloud of witnesses and that their stories are recorded to encourage us and spur us on to live our lives by faith!

It is an awesome thought to realize that others have lived by faith and that their stories tell us we are to do the same! When you think about faith and the kinds of faith you have seen, I know you must wonder how you can really live your life in faith. Well, in Layer Two, you will see what Hebrews 12 says about how to do that!

LAYER TWO: The Race of Life

I think it is super neat that the lives of these heroes of faith are recorded so that we will be encouraged today to live by faith! Do you want to live in a way that will encourage others to live by faith as well?

Truth Trackers: Heroes of Faith

There is treasure hidden in the verses you will dig through in this layer that will help in understanding how to live by faith. If you uncover these treasures and decide to live by them, then your life can be an example of faith and make others want to live by faith, too!

1. Read Hebrews 12:2-3.

²fixing our eyes on Jesus, the author and perfecter of faith, who for the joy set before Him endured the cross, despising the shame, and has sat down at the right hand of the throne of God.
   ³For consider Him who has endured such hostility by sinners against Himself, so that you will not grow weary and lose heart. (Hebrews 12:2-3)

2. Write below the first three words of verse 2.

3. Now, write out the first three words of verse 3.

4. Now think about what you are told to do in these verses.

5. The two verses tell you more about Jesus, don't they? But you are told to do two things. You are to:

• Fix your eyes on Jesus   • Consider Jesus

6. Now, let's read all of Hebrews 12:1-3 at the same time. As you read, think about the two things in verse 1 that you are told to do, and also think about the two things in verses 2 and 3 that you just discovered you are to do.

¹Therefore, since we have so great a cloud of witnesses surrounding us, let us also lay aside every encumbrance and the sin which so easily entangles us, and let us run with endurance the race that is set before us, ²fixing our eyes on Jesus, the author and perfecter of faith, who for the joy set before Him endured the cross, despising the shame, and has sat down at the right hand of the throne of God.
   ³For consider Him who has endured such hostility by sinners against Himself, so that you will not grow weary and lose heart. (Hebrews 12:1-3)

WOW! Let's see what you just read!
  • There is a cloud of witnesses who lived life by faith.
  • Life is like a race and to run it well you must live in faith.

Jesus: Author and Perfecter of OUR Faith

- In order to live by faith, you have to set aside things that will hold you back.
- AND you have to fix your eyes on Jesus!

Have you ever run a race? First to be sure you run as fast as you can, you trim back things you don't need. You don't wear your sweats, you wear shorts and a T-shirt! You don't strap on your hiking boots like you wear on our digs! You put on your lightweight running shoes, don't you? And when you run the race, you don't look at the person to your right or to your left. You look toward the ribbon, the goal. So, when you run the race of life, you set aside things that will hold you back and you look at Jesus—because your goal is to be like Him!

What an amazing find! Think about it!

LAYER THREE: The Big Plan

In Hebrews 12:2-3, there are some important truths about Jesus to uncover. Let's dig them out!

1. Go back and read Hebrews 12:2-3 in Layer Two. Underline in red everything you see that tells you about Jesus or about something He did.

2. Now, let's take out what you have uncovered and look more closely at the truths. Take your time and fill in the spaces I have left for you. These will help you see the things Hebrews 12:2-3 tell you about Jesus and give you a closer look!

the _____ and _____ of our faith

for the ____ ____ _____ ____ endured the cross, despising the shame

has sat down at the _____ _____ of the _____ of _____

has endured such _____ by _____

3. To help you understand what you have discovered, I think we need to go back and think about a truth you found in Dig Three when you looked at Abel's faith.

Do you remember that when Adam and Eve sinned God made garments for them? Can you remember why? Write what you recall.

4. Yes, Adam and Eve were ashamed and realized that they were naked. God made garments to cover their shame. What kind of garment did He make?

5. Right again. He made garments from animal skins. I think you may even remember why since it is such an amazing reason. But, in case you don't, read the verse below and then write why God made animal skins for Adam and Eve.

And according to the Law, one may almost say, all things are cleansed with blood, and without shedding of blood there is no forgiveness. (Hebrews 9:22)

Yes, that is it! Because without the shedding of blood there would be no forgiveness. Without the blood shed, the sin would not be covered.

BIG PLAN

6. Do you also remember that this plan God put in place to cover man's sin was a temporary plan? We talked about the fact that there was a BIG PLAN He would put in place one day that would take man's sin away! When the Big Plan was in place, the sin would not just be covered temporarily—it would be covered once for all time!

7. On page 158 there is a fun puzzle for you to try your hand at! Have fun!

Well, Jesus was a part of the plan for taking sin away. How and why He did this are all a part of what Hebrews 12:2-3 is talking about. I know you are eager to know more, but let's take a break. In Layer Four, we will begin to dig and see why Jesus could cover sin for all time and how He would do it! Meet me there soon.

LAYER FOUR: Sin Covered for All Time!

We are digging today to find out why Jesus was able take away man's sin. And we also want to understand how He did it. So, let's not waste any time!

1. Let's dig into two verses from another chapter in the book of Hebrews.

Jesus: Author and Perfecter of OUR Faith

14Therefore, since the children share in flesh and blood, He Himself likewise also partook of the same, that through death He might render powerless him who had the power of death, that is, the devil, **15**and might free those who through fear of death were subject to slavery all their lives. (Hebrews 2:14-15)

The verse says that children (mankind) are made of flesh and blood. So Jesus, who was the Son of God, came to earth in the form of man—flesh and blood. You see, don't you, that Jesus became a man so that He could be like mankind?

2. Can you see that the devil held the power of death? That is scary, isn't it? Read verse 14 again and write what it says about the devil.

3. What does verse 14 say that Jesus is going to do for mankind?

Yes, it says He is going to die for them!

4. Why did Jesus need to die for mankind? Read Romans 6:23 and see what you find about the wages—or cost—of sin. Write what you see below.

For the wages of sin is death, but the free gift of God is eternal life in Christ Jesus our Lord. (Romans 6:23)

5. Sin brought with it a cost. Because man sinned, he would now die. But God had a BIG PLAN! He did not want man to die spiritually or physically. God did not want man to be separated from Him. What is the gift that God is giving man?

6. Remember that when animals were killed to cover sin that only the one sin was covered. Another animal had to die to cover more sin. Then another animal had to die to cover more sin. And on and on it went. The cycle never stopped! There was sin, and an animal had to die!
But when Jesus died, His blood covered man's sin—once and for all time! His blood took the power of sin away. Jesus paid the price that was needed to take away the penalty of sin!

Read Hebrews 9:28 and write how many times Jesus was offered for sin.

so Christ also, having been offered once to bear the sins of many, will appear a second time for salvation without *reference to* sin, to those who eagerly await Him.
(Hebrews 9:28)

7. Man was supposed to die because the penalty of sin is death. But God gave man the gift of eternal life. He gave this gift when Jesus died on the cross and shed His blood to cover mankind's sin. Since your sin has been covered once for all, you do not have to be separated from God—now or after your body dies!

Go back and read Romans 6:23 again and write below how much the gift of eternal will cost you.

8. You can have the gift of eternal life—salvation—free! Do you know how you take the gift? Read the verse below and see how you can accept this gift.

Therefore having been justified by faith, we have peace with God through our Lord Jesus Christ. (Romans 5:1)

Yes, it is by faith!

CLUE # 4: To be justified means that you will be in a right relationship with God because the sin that separates you from Him is covered! Write below how you accept the gift of eternal life.

Now take a breath after all the hard digging you have done! Sit back and think about Rahab's faith. It was a faith that believed God could save her form the destruction that was coming, wasn't it? And that is the kind of faith it takes to accept this gift that God gives.

Do you believe that your sin has been covered by Jesus' blood? Do you believe that the penalty of your sin has been taken away? These are very important questions. They are the most important questions anyone can ever ask you. You should talk with your mom or dad about these questions.

I will pray for you as you think about these questions and as you talk with someone about them!

Jesus: Author and Perfecter of OUR Faith

LAYER FIVE: Jesus Sat Down and...

Do you wonder what Jesus is doing now since He has already come to earth as man and paid the price for your sin by shedding His blood? It is a good question. Let's see what you can dig out to answer it.

1. Read Hebrews 8:1. Jesus is referred to as a "high priest" in this verse, so you will know the verse is talking about Him when you see this title. What do you see Jesus did after He died and rose from the dead?

> Now the main point in what has been said *is this*: we have such a high priest, who has taken His seat at the right hand of the throne of the Majesty in the heavens.
> (Hebrews 8:1)

2. Where did He sit down?

3. Can you think about who is called "the Majesty" in this verse? Write what you think.

If you said God, you are correct.

4. Read Hebrews 1:3. You will see some of the same treasures, but in this verse, you will see when Jesus sat down. Write exactly what the verse says.

> And He is the radiance of His glory and the exact representation of His nature, and upholds all things by the word of His power. When He had made purification of sins, He sat down at the right hand of the Majesty on high. (Hebrews 1:3)

When Jesus finished the job He had been given to do on earth, He sat down at the right hand of God's throne in heaven! In this verse, the words used to say He finished His job are "when He made purification of sins." It means when Jesus covered your sin and made a way for you to be pure or clean from sin!

5. Read Hebrews 7:25 on the next page to see what Jesus does while He sits at God's right hand. Write it down. It is an awesome find!

Therefore He is able also to save forever those who draw near to God through Him, since He always lives to make intercession for them. (Hebrews 7:25)

6. Do you know what "intercession" is? It is prayer! Jesus is praying for you! How long will He pray for you?

He ever lives to pray for you! He will pray for you from now on! That is awesome!

7. Let's look at more verses and then you have reached the bottom! Hard to believe you are almost to the bottom of this dig on faith, isn't it?

31"Simon, Simon, behold, Satan has demanded *permission* to sift you like wheat; **32**but I have prayed for you, that your faith may not fail; and you, when once you have turned again, strengthen your brothers." (Luke 22:31-32)

When Jesus was still on earth and was talking to Peter (also called Simon and one of His disciples whom He loved very much), He told Peter that He would pray for him. Peter was having a hard time, and he was discouraged and confused. So, Jesus was going to pray for Peter. What exactly did He say He would pray?

Aren't you encouraged to know that Jesus is praying for you! Not only did He die so that you could have eternal life, He is praying that your faith will not fail! He wants you to make it. He wants you to run the race well!

Jesus wants you to have a strong faith that will abandon itself to Him and obey, trust, and believe, and be patient, confident, steadfast, devoted, and fearless. And He is praying!

Now that should knock your socks off and leave your bare feet sitting in your shoes! That is how exciting this awesome truth is!

Can you see why Jesus is called the author and perfecter of your faith? He died to make a way for you to have faith in Him and be free from sin. That is how He is the author. And He is praying for you that your faith will not fail. That is how He is the perfecter!

I, too, pray that you will make the choices that will lead you into a life of faith. I, too, pray that you will make choices that will make you a man or woman of great faith— the kind God can honor!

Truth Treasures for the Week

1.

2.

3.

Bury the Treasure:

For you are all sons of God through faith in Jesus Christ (Galatians 3:24).

Truth Trackers: Heroes of Faith

Mystery Maze

Find your way through the maze to discover a hidden message! Trace a path from start to finish using a pencil. When you've made it to the finish, go back and erase any wrong turns you may have made, then color in the correct path. The answer will reveal the words to the topic of our study. Good luck!

solution on page 168

Treasure Map

Hebrews 11:1–12:3

Chapter 11:

1 Now faith is the assurance of *things* hoped for, the conviction of things not seen. **2** For by it the men of old gained approval.

3 By faith we understand that the worlds were prepared by the word of God, so that what is seen was not made out of things which are visible.

4 By faith Abel offered to God a better sacrifice than Cain, through which he obtained the testimony that he was righteous, God testifying about his gifts, and through faith, though he is dead, he still speaks. **5** By faith Enoch was taken up so that he would not see death; and he was not found because God took him up; for he obtained the witness that before his being taken up he was pleasing to God. **6** And without faith it is impossible to please *Him*, for he who comes to God must believe that He is and *that* He is a rewarder of those who seek Him. **7** By faith Noah, being warned *by God* about things not yet seen, in reverence prepared an ark for the salvation of his household, by which he condemned the world, and became an heir of the righteousness which is according to faith.

8 By faith Abraham, when he was called, obeyed by going out to a place which he was to receive for an inheritance; and he went out, not knowing where he was going. **9** By faith he lived as an alien in the land of promise, as in a foreign *land*, dwelling in tents with Isaac and Jacob, fellow heirs of the same promise; **10** for he was looking for the city which has foundations, whose architect and builder is God. **11** By faith even Sarah herself received ability to conceive, even beyond the proper time of life, since she considered Him faithful who had promised. **12** Therefore there was born even of one man, and him as good as dead at that, *as many descendants* as the stars of heaven in number, and innumerable as the sand which is by the seashore.

13 All these died in faith, without receiving the promises, but having seen them and having welcomed them from a distance, and having confessed that they were strangers and exiles on the earth. **14**For those who say such things make it clear that they are seeking a country of their own. **15**And indeed if they had been thinking of that *country* from which they went out, they would have had opportunity to return. **16**But as it is, they desire a better *country*, that is, a heavenly one. Therefore God is not ashamed to be called their God; for He has prepared a city for them.

17By faith Abraham, when he was tested, offered up Isaac, and he who had received the promises was offering up his only begotten *son*; **18***it was he* to whom it was said, "In Isaac your descendants shall be called." **19**He considered that God is able to raise *people* even from the dead, from which he also received him back as a type. **20**By faith Isaac blessed Jacob and Esau, even regarding things to come. **21**By faith Jacob, as he was dying, blessed each of the sons of Joseph, and worshiped, *leaning* on the top of his staff. **22**By faith Joseph, when he was dying, made mention of the exodus of the sons of Israel, and gave orders concerning his bones.

23By faith Moses, when he was born, was hidden for three months by his parents, because they saw he was a beautiful child; and they were not afraid of the king's edict. **24**By faith Moses, when he had grown up, refused to be called the son of Pharaoh's daughter, **25**choosing rather to endure ill-treatment with the people of God than to enjoy the passing pleasures of sin, **26**considering the reproach of Christ greater riches than the treasures of Egypt; for he was looking to the reward. **27**By faith he left Egypt, not fearing the wrath of the king; for he endured, as seeing Him who is unseen. **28**By faith he kept the Passover and the sprinkling of the blood, so that he who destroyed the firstborn would not touch them. **29**By faith they passed through the Red Sea as though *they were passing* through dry land; and the Egyptians, when they attempted it, were drowned.

30By faith the walls of Jericho fell down after they had been encircled for seven days. **31**By faith Rahab the harlot did not perish along with those who were disobedient, after she had welcomed the spies in peace.

32And what more shall I say? For time will fail me if I tell of Gideon, Barak, Samson, Jephthah, of David and Samuel and the prophets, **33**who by faith conquered kingdoms, performed *acts of* righteousness, obtained promises, shut the mouths of lions, **34**quenched the power of fire, escaped the edge of the sword, from weakness were made strong, became mighty in war, put foreign armies to flight. **35**Women received *back* their dead by resurrection; and others were tortured, not accepting their release, so that they might obtain a better resurrection; **36**and others experienced mockings and scourgings, yes, also chains and imprisonment. **37**They were stoned, they were sawn in two, they were tempted, they were put to death with the sword; they went about in sheepskins, in goatskins, being destitute, afflicted, ill-treated **38**(*men* of whom the world was not worthy), wandering in deserts and mountains and caves and holes in the ground.

39And all these, having gained approval through their faith, did not receive what was promised, **40**because God had provided something better for us, so that apart from us they would not be made perfect.

Chapter 12:

1Therefore, since we have so great a cloud of witnesses surrounding us, let us also lay aside every encumbrance and the sin which so easily entangles us, and let us run with endurance the race that is set before us, **2**fixing our eyes on Jesus, the author and perfecter of faith, who for the joy set before Him endured the cross, despising the shame, and has sat down at the right hand of the throne of God.

3For consider Him who has endured such hostility by sinners against Himself, so that you will not grow weary and lose heart.

Key to Games

Search and Decipher on page 19

```
S A O * G M O S E S
R B * E A T * A A *
C E N O C H * R L O
U L D O * F W A * I
T * N A B R A H A M
E S * J * A * S E S
J O S E P H S * U R
R * O S D A V I D *
U N * U * B D * I N
* G U S * S N O A H
```

"...SO GREAT A CLOUD OF WITNESSES SURROUNDING US..."

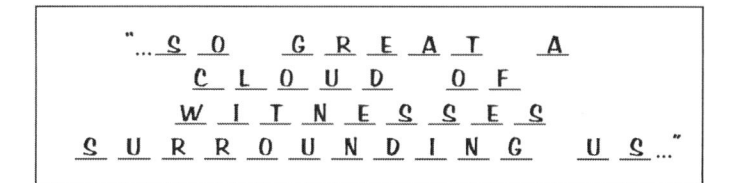

Missing Pieces Puzzle on page 33

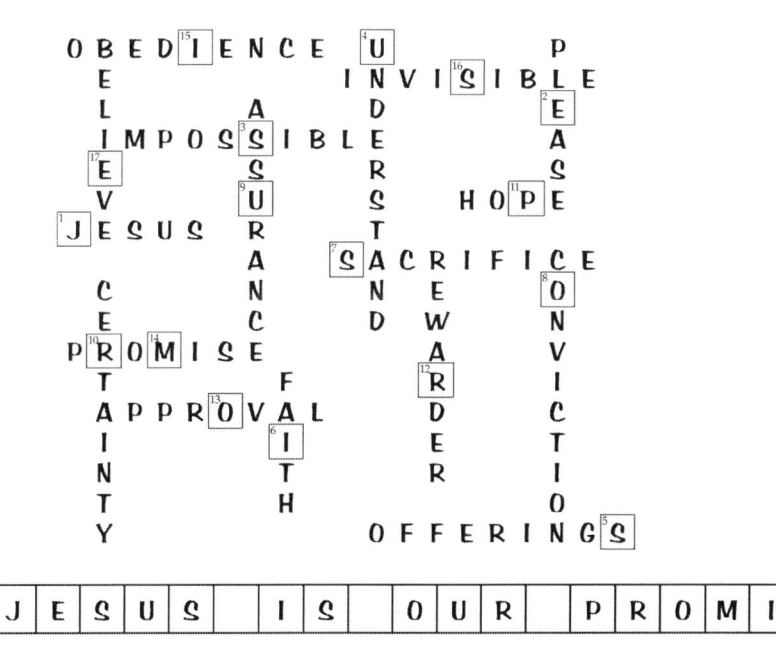

```
    O B E D I E N C E    U         P
    E                 I N V I S I B L E
    L                    D        E
    I M P O S S I B L E  E         A
    E           U        R         S
    V           R    H O P E       
    J E S U S   A        T         
    C           N   S A C R I F I C E
    E           C    E             O
    P R O M I S E    W             N
    C           F    A             V
    A P P R O V A L  R             I
    I           I    D             C
    N           T                  T
    T           H                  I
    Y                O F F E R I N G S
```

```
J E S U S   I S   O U R   P R O M I S E
```

Maze Puzzler on page 45

To obey is better than...

S A C R I F I C E

Hidden Truths on page 55

1. B̶E̶N̶X̶O̶C̶H̶W̶A̶L̶K̶E̶D̶W̶I̶T̶H̶G̶O̶D̶

   Hidden Truth: _Enoch walked with God._

2. H̶E̶Z̶E̶K̶I̶A̶H̶P̶R̶A̶Y̶E̶D̶A̶N̶D̶W̶A̶S̶H̶E̶A̶L̶E̶D̶

   Hidden Truth: _Hezekiah prayed and was healed._

3. M̶I̶C̶A̶H̶S̶P̶O̶K̶E̶T̶O̶T̶H̶E̶P̶E̶O̶P̶L̶E̶O̶F̶G̶O̶D̶

   Hidden Truth: _Micah spoke to the people of God._

Key to Games

Noah Crossword Puzzle on page 68

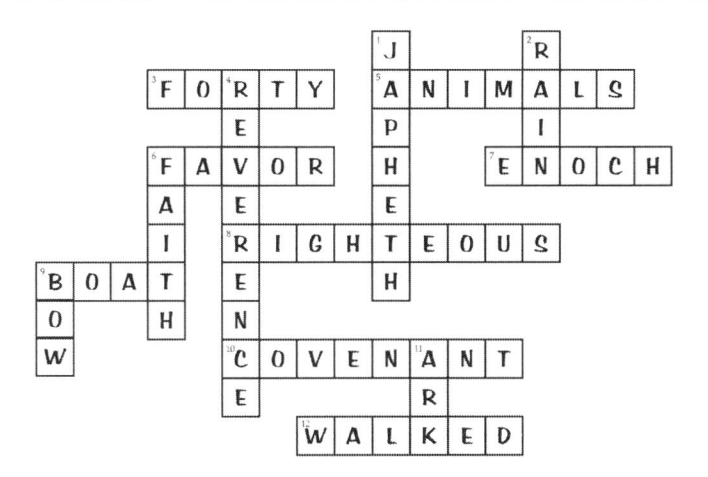

Across:
3. FORTY
5. ANIMALS
6. FAVOR
7. ENOCH
8. RIGHTEOUS
9. BOAT
10. COVENANT
12. WALKED

Down:
1. JAPHETH
2. RII (RAIN)
4. ORE... (REGENERATION — as shown: R, E, G, E, N, E)
5. SHEM (AHI... spelled down)
6. FAITH
9. BOW
11. ARK

A Constellation Promise on page 81

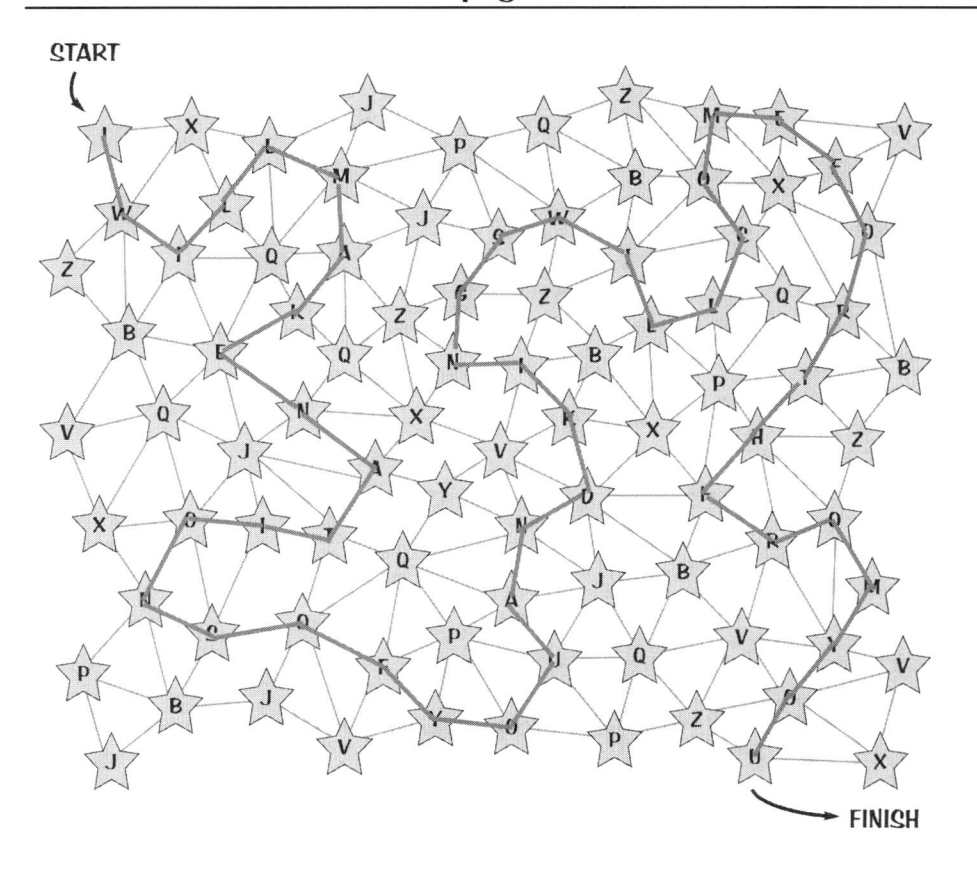

"I WILL MAKE NATIONS OF YOU, AND KINGS WILL COME FORTH FROM YOU."

See Genesis 10:6.

Truth Trackers: Heroes of Faith

An Alphanumber Promise on page 90

I	S		A	N	Y	T	H	I	N G
	T	O	O		D	I	F	F	I C
U	L	T		F	O	R		T	H E
	L	O	R	D	?	...	A	T	T
H	I	S		T	I	M	E	N	E
X	T		Y	E	A	R	...	S	A R
A	H		W	I	L	L		H	A V
E		A		S	O	N		Genesis 18:14	

"IS ANYTHING TOO DIFFICULT FOR THE LORD? ...
AT THIS TIME NEXT YEAR ... SARAH WILL HAVE A SON."

Name Game on page 106

1. B O A J C — J A C O B
2. A H A R H O P — P H A R O A H
3. R A B E K — B A K E R
4. O H S J E P — J O S E P H
5. A P I O T P H R — P O T I P H A R
6. J E B N A N I M — B E N J A M I N
7. E B A R C U R P E — C U P B E A R E R
8. U B E N E R — R E U B E N
9. H U D J A — J U D A H

"THE LORD WAS WITH HIM;
AND WHATEVER HE DID, THE
LORD MADE TO PROSPER."
(Genesis 39:23)

Connect the Dots on page 120

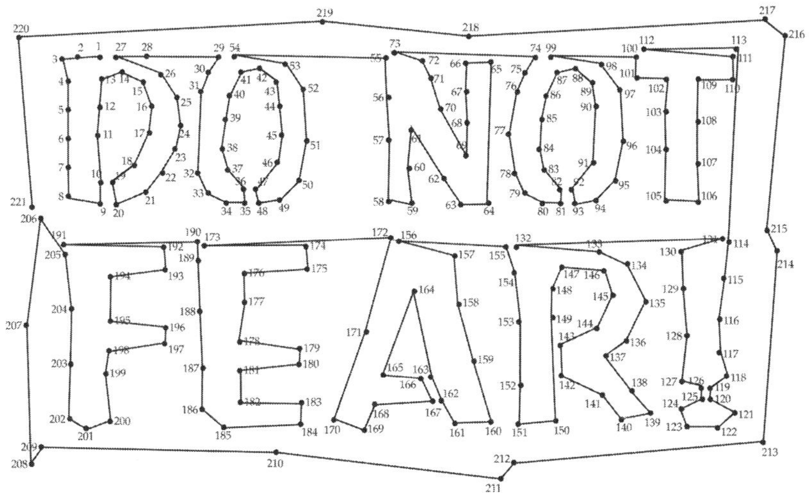

Rahab's Lifeline on page 132

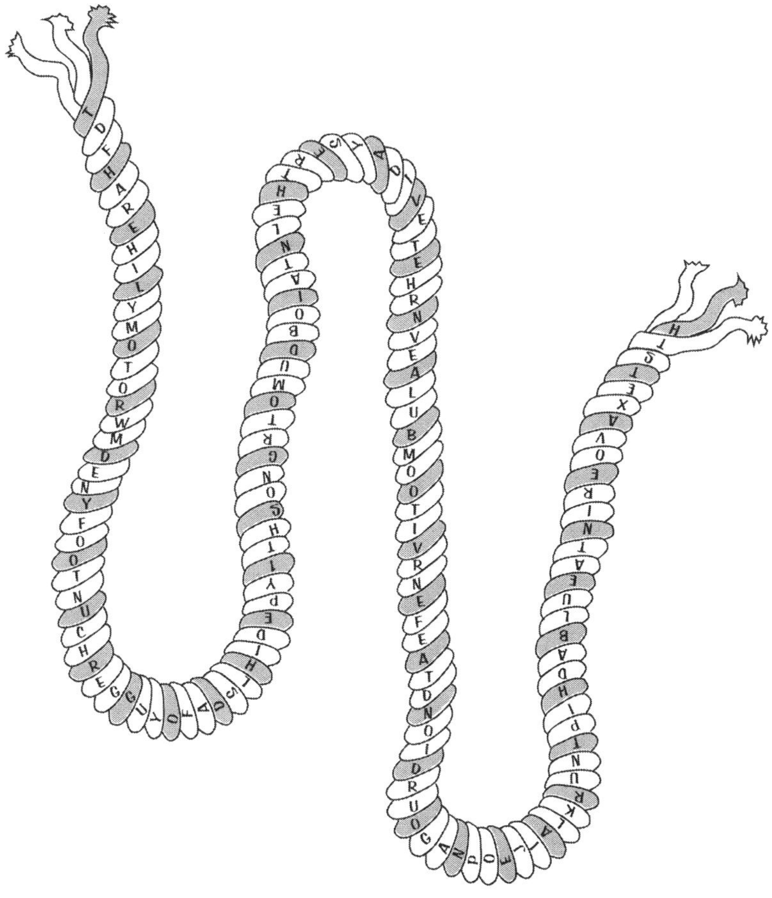

"...THE LORD YOUR GOD, HE IS GOD IN HEAVEN ABOVE AND ON EARTH BENEATH."

(Joshua 2:11)

Truth Trackers: Heroes of Faith

Search and Decipher 2 on page 146

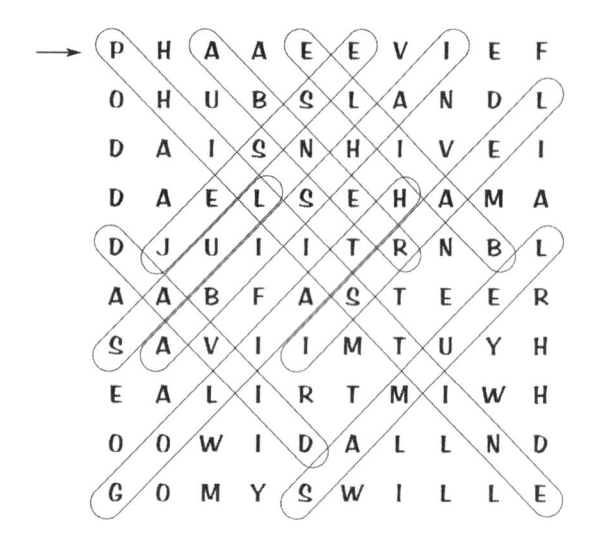

"I HAVE FOUND DAVID...
A MAN AFTER MY HEART,
WHO WILL DO...MY WILL."

(Acts 13:22)

Mystery Maze on page 158